T0304854

LIGHTNING CAN STRIKE TWICE

My Life as a Fury

TOMMY FURY

SPHERE

SPHERE

First published in Great Britain in 2024 by Sphere

1 3 5 7 9 10 8 6 4 2

A CIP catalogue record for this book
is available from the British Library.

Hardback ISBN 978-1-4087-3226-7
Trade paperback ISBN 978-1-4087-3227-4

Typeset in Sabon by M Rules
Printed and bound in Great Britain by
Clays Ltd, Elcograf S.p.A

Papers used by Sphere are from well-managed forests
and other responsible sources.

MIX
Paper | Supporting
responsible forestry
FSC
www.fsc.org   FSC® C104740

Sphere
An imprint of
Little, Brown Book Group
Carmelite House
50 Victoria Embankment
London EC4Y 0DZ

An Hachette UK Company
www.hachette.co.uk

www.littlebrown.co.uk

To Molly and Bambi, my world

Contents

Prologue

I was in the boxing ring on my own.

The venue was crammed with noisy people, the air heavy with anticipation and excitement. It was hard to concentrate. Everyone was impatient for the action to start, hungry for blood, sweat and humiliation. I could see my family – my brothers Tyson, Shane and Roman, my Uncle Peter and Cousin Hughie – sitting at a table within spitting distance of me. My body was shaking uncontrollably; I couldn't stop it moving as the adrenalin pumped through me. I had never felt like this before, and I had no idea what to do with these emotions in such a public space.

Here I stood, the youngest in a long line of Fury fighting men. Boxing may have been in my blood, but I was in the ring because of me. This is what I had been working hard towards and focusing on for most of my young life. I had sacrificed so much to be here for this, my dream, and now everything was riding on the next ten minutes.

I was fifteen years old, and this was my first fight.

It was Friday, a school day, and the hours I'd spent leading up to the fight had been powered by nerves and anxiety. They coursed through me as I went from lesson to lesson, unable to listen to a single word the teachers said. All I could think about was what was to come. Over and over, I ran through the scenarios in my head, rehearsing my combinations and footwork, ignoring fractions and French verbs. My stomach was in a tight knot, and I couldn't face eating lunch – I just counted down the slow hours until I could leave. I didn't tell anyone at school about my plans for the evening because, God forbid, what if the worst happened? What if I lost?

When I got home, I dumped my school bag and sat on my bed, momentarily frozen by the fear of what was to come. I knew I really needed to pull myself together or I would be fit for nothing. I stared at a jacket potato smothered with cheese and beans, forcing forkfuls into my mouth without tasting it, and left the rest when the nerves got the better of me. I tried to watch a film to take my mind off the evening and stop me checking the time every few minutes. Then my dad rang. He had been training me before he was sent to prison and now, he was calling me from there, in his allotted time slot. He ran through the fight with me.

'No matter what happens, box how YOU box.' His voice sounded so close, I knew he would be with me in spirit. 'I know what you are capable of, so go out there and surprise everyone.' I thanked him, but I didn't tell him how much I wished he could be with me because that wasn't helpful for either of us.

My coach and mentor, Tommy Battle – the man with the best name in boxing – came to pick me up at about 6 p.m. and I suppressed my nerves, remaining outwardly calm although my stomach was doing somersaults. I trained with Tommy at the Team Fury Gym on Halliwell Road in Bolton, and he was the one who had decided I was ready for my first amateur fight. Tommy drove me to the Mahdlo Centre in Oldham while I sat in the back of the car with my headphones on listening to Eminem's 'Lose Yourself' on repeat. It was like Eminem was talking directly to me, telling me this was my one shot, my chance, the opportunity of a lifetime. I was trying to get into 'the zone', but I had no idea what that was or how to find it because I had never done this before. I had nothing to compare it to.

In the changing room, I got dressed in my kit. I was proud to wear the blue vest with the Team Fury logo on the left and the name of my amateur boxing club,

Metro ABC, on the right. I borrowed the long white shorts, which had Metro on the waistband, from the gym and my mum had bought me a pair of white, blue and red Lonsdale boots a couple of weeks earlier so I could break them in. I looked like a boxer, even if I was struggling to feel like one. I stood, fists raised, posing for a photograph and I thought, This is it, there is no going back. I come from a fighting family, the youngest of six boys. I couldn't let anyone down and I didn't want to be the one to spoil the name. There was so much weight on my young shoulders and yet in that moment a sense of calm came over me. I knew it was pointless to overthink everything just before I went in the ring, I had to do what I could do, so I put my gloves on and got warmed up on the pads. It was right there and then that I found the zone and was truly in it, throwing the punches and fighting for my life in the changing room.

I was in one of around ten amateur fights happening that night and was put on later in the schedule, in a really good slot. That was what my name did for me. It created an expectation and a curiosity that I had to work my hardest to live up to. But the name could also slow me down. After I was carded (passing a medical to say I was fit to box), it took over six months to set up my first fight because interested opponents kept dropping out. Every so often we would get a confirmed fight, then it would be called off, and we would be back to the drawing board. Everyone knew the family reputation and the name, so it put a few amateur boxers off – even though I hadn't yet been in the ring. There was already a rumour that I was tough, and I was physically bigger than a lot of boys my own age. While Fury was a big name in the boxing world, thanks to Tyson, nobody really knew much about me, his little brother.

Just before I started the ring walk, I pushed back the curtains behind the glass wall of the leisure centre to take a look, and the place was packed to the rafters. I had only ever sparred in front of fifteen people maximum, and now I would have to go out and fight in front of more than three hundred tough critics. The audience was mostly made up of the family and friends of the twenty or so boxers who were fighting that night. Goose bumps spread over my entire body. I was living the Eminem line about sweaty palms, weak knees and heavy arms, but there was no doubt in my mind. Now I was there, I never once thought that I couldn't do it. There was no danger of me backing out, I really wanted to impress everyone and that was what propelled me through the throng of people.

'In the blue corner is Tommy Fury, making his amateur debut!'

The introduction rang out across the crowd to

cheers and the chanting of 'FURY!' and suddenly there I was in the ring. Minutes felt like hours while I waited for my opponent to come out. I didn't know if the delay was a tactic or not. He was a year older than me, and it was his first fight too, so neither of us knew what we were facing, but I sure as hell knew all eyes would be on me. At that point, Tyson was the British Commonwealth and European boxing champion, so some people were there in the hope that he would turn up, and they weren't disappointed. One of Tyson's training partners, Eddie Chambers, who was also a big name in boxing, was there too, so I was aware of how many skilled people were in the audience. The pressure of comparison and success has always been present.

When my opponent stepped into the ring, I thought, I can do this. He was a normal build with less muscle than me, so I just knew by looking at him. Besides, I had no option but to win. I had been training and hoping for this opportunity for as long as I could re-member, from a small boy watching my dad on the punchbag to a proud brother of a boxing champ; I wanted in on the action. My opponent was nothing in the face of this. I almost felt sorry for him. Waiting for the bell was exactly like you see in the films and as I imagined it would be. The other boxer had a lot more support on the night than I did. He wasn't from a boxing family, but he had all his friends there raising the roof for him. I hadn't asked anyone other than my uncle and brothers. My mum refused to come because she couldn't sit and watch me being hit and as for my dad, well, you know where he was. Our earlier telephone conversation flashed through my mind and I pushed away the feeling of longing for him to be by my side. I could do this – after all, I was used to him being absent by this stage.

The bell rang and the jangling feeling of nausea and butterflies inside me disappeared instantly, like magic. It was a split second, as if somebody had clicked their fingers and I had woken up in my old gym, sparring with my usual boys, and nobody was watching me. The fear evaporated and taking its place came the fire. Beast mode was activated. In the first round, I dominated for the full two minutes, landing all my shots exactly as I had dreamed about. It was perfect. He was taking it. I was coming from every angle, and he didn't have an answer. It may have been just a trial amateur fight for him, but I had everything on the line. My family name. My future. My pride. I thought about my dad sitting in jail, watching the clock and willing me on. I was fighting for it all and I wasn't going down.

In the second round my opponent still couldn't get out of the way of my shots. I gave him a bloody nose.

When I knew I could have my way I began to give it more gas. I don't remember him touching me, I don't think he had a chance. The bell went and my coach, Tommy, jumped up into the ring and urged me on, saying I had to keep using my jab, put my right hand behind it and keep my head moving.

'You are winning this fight,' he said, slapping me on the back encouragingly. That was all I needed to hear.

In the third round, I knew how to judge the action and the level of my opponent's power, and I was sure he wouldn't be able to hurt me. I could land shots at will and any energy I had been saving could now be spent in these final two minutes. I hit him with my right hand and his head went through the ropes. The referee, smart in his white shirt and bow tie, put his arm out to pause the fight and sent me to the neutral corner. He started counting one . . . two . . . three . . . I was amazed. I couldn't believe it. This was better than I could have wished for. Just in time, my opponent recovered so the fight didn't get stopped and it went to points, but having that standing eight count validated every torturous training session, early morning run and the countless bruises.

The crowd went mad, clapping and cheering as we went to our corners. The look on Tommy's face told me I had done it, but I knew not to celebrate too soon. We came back into the middle of the ring and then the referee raised my arm, declaring me the winner by unanimous decision. Now I could let go. Someone caught this moment on camera, and when I look at that photo now, it transports me straight back to the way I felt; the expression on my face says it all. I was roaring like a lion; I was unstoppable. It was as if I had just fought for millions of pounds rather than an amateur fight in a sweaty leisure centre. If I had been asked to choose between winning the lottery or the high I had just experienced, I would not have picked the money. Clutching a plastic trophy cup in front of my grinning family, I gained something invaluable that night. I knew without doubt that this was my whole world and that I had legitimately earned my place in it.

My coach was as proud of me as my family were. They all hugged me and made a big old fuss, it was the most amazing feeling and everything I imagined it would be. I knew winning this fight would take me to the next one and so on. This was the life I had chosen, and I wanted to hurry it up, move forward and achieve greatness because I knew this was my answer to the future. I wanted to prove to myself and everyone else that my single-minded focus was worth it. Imagine getting up at 4 a.m. to run, training every night, putting in all this effort, only to go out there and lose. This guy is crazy, people would say, and he's not even any good.

Back in the changing room, I rang my mum. She was screaming with relief and excitement down the phone. I called my nana too and she reacted in exactly the same way. I think they had both been holding their breath for the last hour. Everyone was over the moon. I didn't speak to Dad until the following morning when he was allowed to make a call again. I went to bed that night with the phone on my bedside table because I knew he would ring first thing. When he did, I answered immediately.

'Go on then, tell me,' he said.

'I won, Dad, and I got a standing eight count.'

'I told you, you could do it! Proud of you, Son. I can't wait to see you fight when I get out.' He was really chuffed and that meant so much. The final validation.

I can step back into the memory of the night and experience every detail of it. I can feel the sweat trickling down my back, sense the exhilaration in the crowd and see my opponent on the ropes. That fight set up everything for me. If I had lost, I am not sure I would have been quite so ready to get back out there or put my family through the risk of losing again. Tyson said I looked like a professional in the ring and his praise echoed in my ears for days after.

This was just the start for me, and it made me hungry for what would be next. I had no idea what the future had in store then, the twists and turns that were to come, the number of times my life would come full circle and the way my career would leap from something so familiar into a world beyond my wildest imagination. Had someone told me then, I would not have believed them – even though it was what I wished for. Nor would I have truly understood that with the soaring highs come the crashing lows and how my toughest opponent would turn out to be myself. This was all to come.

Right here, right now, I was on a quest to carve out my own path in the wake of Tyson's career. I wasn't sure this was even possible, and I don't think my family and friends thought so either. One success in the family was already a surprise for people like us, but two? That was plain greedy. Yet I had just won my first fight and it made me wonder whether lightning can strike in the same place twice . . .

1

The Sixth Fury

*Boxing has always been in me. Ever since
I was very young, when I started tapping
around and hitting my dad's hands, it has
been there for me. I grew up in the gym,
training with my brothers and cousins.*

My nana told me about the night I was born.
Apparently, there was a huge storm with flashes of
lightning, deafening rumbles of thunder and a terrible blizzard. She said she had never experienced an
evening like it as she made her way to Salford Royal
Hospital to see me. It was strange because it was May,
a month not known for really bad weather conditions.
Nana said I entered the world – in the early hours of

7 May 1999 – with my face scrunched up and my fists raised, as if I was ready to box right there and then. She laughed and told me I looked like St James; I didn't know who she meant so I googled him recently, and up came one of the twelve apostles of Jesus. On the internet, St James is depicted as a man with bushy eyebrows and a big beard. Thanks for that, Nana!

I am of mixed heritage. Half of me is Gypsy on my dad John's side and I am a quarter Mauritian and a quarter English on my mum Chantal's. That's an estimate, not an exact measurement, because I think there is some Irish and French thrown in there somewhere too. Whatever I am, I am proud of it all. I know being a Traveller and living in a house confuses people. Just because Dad settled, rather than moving around the country in a caravan, doesn't make him less of a Traveller. It's in his DNA and it's in mine too; it's something you are born into, you can't become it even if you spent the rest of your life on the road. That's not how it works. You either are or you are not, wherever you choose to wake up in the morning.

When Mum and Dad got together, he had been married before and had four boys already. I think one of their earliest dates involved her going to the gym to watch him box, so no surprises there. They had my brother Roman, and two and a half years later, I made my big entrance in the middle of a raging storm.

I was christened Thomas John Fury, the youngest of the Fury boys. The order goes John Boy, Tyson, Shane, Hughie, Roman and me. While Roman and I have a different mum from the rest, we consider our older siblings as full brothers, and they feel the same way. There is nothing 'half' about our relationships: we are all as one.

It sounds a bit of a cliché to say I had a happy childhood, but I really did. I grew up in the Traveller ways, with Dad going out every day to earn the money and Mum busy at home – cooking, cleaning and looking after us. Dad would leave the house before 7 a.m. most mornings. He bought and sold cars, making deals and driving across the country. It's a cultural thing for male Travellers to work hard and strive for success in whatever they do, usually running their own business, which is what Dad did. Our bills were always paid on time, we had a good meal on the table every night, there were presents for birthdays and Christmas and we went on holiday. That made a big impression on me growing up because I knew I wanted to provide for my own family too when I had one. It was a very traditional set-up and Roman and I felt safe, secure and loved within it.

As well as great parents, I had fantastic grandparents who formed a supportive ring around us. Dad's father, Huey, must have been one of the only Furys who never used his fists: he hated fighting. We would regularly visit him and my granny, Sissy, in their bungalow in Stockport and she would give us a zip-up bag full of toys and racing cars to play with on the rug. Grandad would be sat in a chair in the corner, and I remember him being incredibly well dressed, wearing a shirt, tie, smart trousers, polished shoes and his hair neatly combed. I was too young to understand how ill he was, and he died of motor neurone disease when I was still small, which was awful for Granny, my dad and his three brothers.

My maternal grandparents have been like second parents to me over the years. Grandad was born and raised in Mauritius, studied to become a nurse and came to England when he was twenty-one. He worked at the hospital in Salford and sent money back to his parents every month. It was there that he met my nana, Manchester-born nurse Barbara, and they got married and had my mum followed by my aunt, Claudia, fourteen years later. Grandad worked hard as a night manager at the same hospital for almost sixty years. His real name is Devraj, but everyone calls him Dev and he is cool with that; it is how he chooses to introduce himself. He is such a likeable guy, loves popping to the pub for a pint and a game of snooker and could never do enough for us all. He and my nana are a proper love story and have always been a huge part of my life. I have an awful lot to thank them for.

Growing up, we lived around the corner from my nana and grandad and were one big noisy family, constantly in and out of each other's houses. It was a set-up that worked for us all. Their house was bigger than ours and we would stay there every weekend. Grandad would take Roman and me to the cinema on Saturdays and, because he is Mauritian, we would occasionally go to see an Indian film with subtitles. As we came out, I would always turn to Roman to ask if he understood what had happened and he would shake his head. Neither of us had a clue what we were watching, but we were just happy to be there with Grandad. When we were a bit older, Grandad taught us so many games – ping pong, snooker, cards – and he was another dad to us. We spent so much time together and formed a special bond.

Sometimes we stayed at Nana and Grandad's for as long as a couple of weeks at a time. It was home from home, and all of us being together under one roof gave me some of my best childhood memories; it really helped shape the family first attitude I have.

Of course, there was only one place we wanted to be at Christmas too, and that was round at Nana and Grandad's. It was the highlight of my year, and continues to be – I love Christmas and I think this stems from all those brilliant family experiences. We would go to my grandparents a few days before; Mum and Nana would cook together while Roman and I played games like 'the floor is lava' and wrestled each other in the front room. We helped put the fairy lights up in the garden and decorated the tree in the house. When we were tiny, we shared a bed with Mum, one on one side, one on the other, and we would wake each other up with excitement on Christmas morning, desperate to go and check our stockings. When we were older and the three of us couldn't fit in the bed, one of us would sleep on the camp bed on the floor. Christmas Day was as traditional as you could get, and none of us would have changed a thing about it. We would wake up too early, open presents, play with the presents while Nana and Mum prepared dinner, then after pudding we would chill and get competitive with card games: rummy, twenty-one or snap. You can imagine how much I wanted to win!

Writing this book has put me in touch with the child I was, and I can look at this small boy with the inquisitive bright blue eyes, with a mix of pride and humour, reliving the great memories that have flooded back. Like when I was six, I knew exactly what I was going to ask Father Christmas for. I had watched the film *Rocky*, and I was obsessed with it. I wanted to live inside the movie. My biggest wish was to dress like Sylvester Stallone's character, Rocky Balboa, so I asked for a leather jacket, a pork-pie hat and a bouncy ball to complete the look. I was also desperate for the same shorts Apollo Creed wore when he fought Rocky – a pair with the stars and stripes of the American flag on them. I couldn't believe my eyes when I got it all. I don't think I wore anything else for months after, and I went to bed in the leather jacket. I wore the shorts instead of pyjamas and even put them on under my school uniform. Mum now jokes that they had to be surgically removed. I love that about six-year-old me! I've never done anything by halves, as you will soon discover. For my first fight in America, in Cleveland, Ohio in 2021, a highly watched fight on a big bill, I wore a version of the Apollo Creed shorts. That was one of several full-circle moments in my life that give me goose bumps when I think about them, along with others I will share later in this book.

We had similar rituals around birthdays as we did Christmas, and I wanted the same celebration every year. I would wake up early and stare at the wall listening out for any signs of movement. As soon as I heard as much as a yawn, I would be straight out of bed and hassling everyone to come downstairs so I could open my presents. In the evening, Mum, Dad, Roman and I went to the bowling alley at the Trafford Centre or the one near us, got the children's ramp out and bowled for a couple of hours before going for a meal. Where we went was my choice. Occasionally I would pretend I wanted a change and we would go to TGI Fridays or Chiquito, but my all-time favourite was Frankie & Benny's in Salford Quays because they gave out goody bags on the door full of colouring books, pencils and jokes. The simple pleasures of being a kid!

I am a big fan of a theme, so Halloween was almost better than birthdays and Christmas. I loved everything about it, and I still do; it is one of my favourite celebrations and a high point in the year. We would carve pumpkins with a scary film on in the background, have cosy nights in, tell ghost stories, visit scare parks and go trick-or-treating. Anything spooky works for me, including themed sweets, snacks and fancy-dress costumes. Years later I bought a Michael Myers costume in New York – my favourite horror film is *Halloween* – and chased my girlfriend, Molly, around the hotel room. I was in my element, but she was not amused! Now, she encourages my Halloween excitement and loves dressing up too, although she always manages to look cute rather than scary.

So far so normal, I reckon. I don't think the early part of my childhood was any different from many other people's, including our family holidays, which involved driving a camper van to Cornwall. Mum struggled with claustrophobia and couldn't get on a plane, so taking a trip to the south-west coast was a good alternative. A few years later, this was replaced by a P&O cruise each summer, organised by Nana and Grandad. We stayed at theirs the night before and then set off really early in the morning for the long drive to Southampton to get on the ship and set sail to the Mediterranean. All of us went: my mum, grandparents, Auntie Claudia and my dad, when he could. It was amazing. Every morning, we would go to the Plaza restaurant for breakfast and then back to our cabin to get swimming trunks on and slather ourselves in sun cream before heading to the loungers next to the Horizon Bar and Grill. It was an all-inclusive holiday which meant as many burgers and helpings of chips as us boys could handle, which was several times a day before we started to feel sick. We were in heaven! It felt so grown-up and exciting to go and get food whenever we fancied and not have to pay for it.

No prizes for guessing what I wasn't as keen on as a boy. Yep, school. I was a bit of a menace, in a cute, mischievous way, but then I suppose I would say that. Being brought up in a family where one parent (my dad) didn't consider school to be a priority meant I never thought it mattered that much either. While I really enjoyed my time at St Luke's Roman Catholic Primary School, I think it was mainly due to me treating it as an opportunity to meet up with my friends and mess about with my best mate, Kyle. We stuck together like glue, me and him, and we are still just as close today; he has always been a big part of my life. After a year or so of being in the same class, the teacher decided we may both benefit from being split up to stop us distracting each other and probably those around us. It didn't ruin our friendship; we just met in the playground for every break and lunchtime then, after school, we would cycle round to each other's houses or head to the park opposite his and mess around on the swings. Our little world was small, safe and worry free, and I was never late home for my tea.

Little did I know, but those primary school years were the best it was going to get for me educationally. I listened to the teacher, did my homework and loved PE, but I felt like I was biding my time. I always knew I was going to be different from the other kids around me. It is a weird thing to try and explain, and I hope this doesn't sound arrogant, but when I was about seven, I remember sitting cross-legged on the carpet with my classmates, in front of the teacher, and thinking, I know I am going to be successful in life. I could feel it, the anticipation, the thrill for what was ahead of me. I never doubted it. I kept hold of that vision and I took it with me everywhere I went. Even when everything has gone against me, I have always told myself that if I kept going, I would get there. I think about the little boy on the carpet, and I don't want to disappoint him.

Sport was my absolute passion during this time – I lived for it. Roman and I played rugby for Langworthy Reds and trained every Tuesday and Thursday after school. To begin with, I had to make do with watching Roman because he was older than me, so I would stand on the sidelines with Mum and Nana. I couldn't wait to be old enough to join in and as soon as I could, I was out there in the muddy throng, intent on the win. We played a match every Sunday morning too, so Nana and Mum would cheer us on and then we'd go back to Nana's house for a hot bath followed by a big fry-up. The simplest and happiest of days!

If someone had asked me then what I was going to be a success in, I would have said rugby. Although that wasn't my first choice. What I really wanted to be was a WWE wrestler, but that was like saying I wanted to be an astronaut or a superhero: it was so out of reach it felt almost impossible. I had no idea how you would even get into it, and it didn't seem like anything that could ever happen to someone like me. It certainly wasn't on the school career advisor's list of suggested job choices. I practised wrestling at every opportunity I got, and would watch hours of it on TV. At home, my brother and I wrestled in the house all the time and we bought blow-up beds for the garden so we could do it outside too. We were that committed to the cause. All we ever wanted to do was throw each other around. It was the same with my school mates. Kyle and I would wrestle on the grass every break time, inviting other pupils to take us on. Funnily enough, we didn't get many takers.

I crossed wrestling off my possible career prospects list without even trying to pursue it and, at the grand old age of eleven, I decided to focus on rugby instead. I didn't consider being a boxer at that point because, although I was at the boxing gym most days and it was what so many of my male relatives did, I didn't take it for granted or assume it would be my future. It was just a hobby and something other members of my family were known for.

My dad didn't encourage me to get in the ring either, but he didn't dissuade me when I started showing an interest. As a little kid, I would watch him go out in the evenings, and one day I asked Mum where he was going; she said he was running. When he came back, he would walk through the house and go outside, and I wondered what he was doing then. One night, I followed him when he got back from his run, and he went into the garage, where he had a big boxing bag and some mittens. He put them on and began to bang away, hitting the bag non-stop. I started to go out running with him and, after a while, I followed him into the garage too and sat and watched him. I loved spending time with him, but I was also fascinated by his routine. To begin with I timed him on the bag and then I started hitting the bag too. In an instant, I got the bug and wanted to do it every day. When I wasn't playing rugby, I would be boxing whenever I could, and if I couldn't do either, I would be watching the *Rocky* films and cheering on Sylvester Stallone as the magnificent boxing role model Rocky Balboa.

As we were both showing an interest, Dad took Roman and me to Sports Direct when Roman was about ten and I was eight. He bought us a pair of yellow Lonsdale boxing gloves each. I will never forget them. When we came home, thrilled with our new kit, Roman and I started sparring in the front room and I ended up with a bloody nose. I was wearing a yellow T-shirt and the front of it turned red, which looked pretty dramatic. I ran into the kitchen and Mum was beside herself, but I wasn't put off. We would spar every day and practise not flinching. It's a lot harder than you might think, but I wouldn't suggest you try – just take it from me. The only way to overcome it is with a lot of experience, and I clearly remember the first time I stopped flinching a few years later. I was training non-stop at this point, a lot more than Roman was because he hadn't yet decided to make it his career, but in the ring, I was still unable to stop the reflex response. My sparring partner threw a punch, and I watched his fist coming towards me as I moved my head to avoid it. I didn't look down and I didn't break eye contact with my opponent. It was a massive breakthrough, and I raced home. I couldn't wait to show Roman what I had learned.

'Roman, spar with me, I have got something to show you!' I wanted to make sure it wasn't just a fluke.

'You've stopped flinching!' he said after we had thrown a few punches. 'How did you do that?!' He couldn't believe it. I could tell he was jealous of my new skill.

Boxing has always been in me. Ever since I was very young, when I started tapping around and hitting my dad's hands, it has been there for me. I grew up in the gym, training with my brothers and cousins. That was when Roman and I saw the rest of our family on our dad's side. We lived in Salford, and they were in Wilmslow, so the gym was our meeting place, and we went there most days. It was also our playground: a place to train together, hang out and then go and get food afterwards. We were a band of brothers.

Looking back on the first ten years of my life, I can

see how lucky I was to have the love and support of a big family. There is no better foundation for a child. We didn't have very much money and I definitely wasn't spoiled, but I wanted for nothing. The best times were when I was with my parents, grandparents, brothers and best mates. That was unbeatable. I didn't need anyone else and, other than sport, had no other interests, but I was happy. I had no idea that what was around the corner was going to shake my little world to its core and threaten to capsize our strong family life.

2

The Prison Years

*All of a sudden, this life was over. The
realisation of what Dad's prison sentence
meant, not just to him but to us too, took
a while to sink in, and when it did, I felt
a sadness I had not experienced in my
young life.*

I was ten when my dad went to prison. One weekend,
Roman and I were watching TV and Dad came home,
about 9 p.m., with scratches on his face and his top
ripped. I remember staring at him in confusion before
Mum instructed us to stay in the front room and not
to move, which was pretty hard to do considering
how Dad had just turned up. I couldn't resist taking

a sneaky peek, and I put my head around the door to see Mum with antiseptic wipes, dabbing at the cuts on Dad's face and cleaning the blood up. He went upstairs for a shower and then he left. Nothing was said.

While we were used to Dad going away for work, I knew something was up after a month or so. This was the longest time he had been absent and the last time we'd seen him he had looked really rough. What on earth was going on?

'Why is Dad away for so long? Where is he working? When will he be home?' I asked Mum. I knew she would be straight with me, but I didn't expect the response I got.

'He got into a fight, and it caused a bit of trouble, so he is on remand, which basically means he is going to be in a sort of prison until his case comes to court, but there is nothing to worry about because he is going to win and will be home very soon.' She seemed pretty sure about that.

'Oh, OK,' I said, 'can I watch telly?' It was a hard and weird concept to get my head around, and I was very young, so it was easier not to think too deeply and I didn't dwell on it. I just waited for him to return.

Mum was incredibly strong. She spent a lot of time on the phone dealing with lawyers and navigating the prison system, but I never saw her cry – she was so good at remaining cheerful and keeping everything going for us. Her calm, measured approach helped me take the situation in my stride. When the court date came around, we were at school. I was excited at the thought that Dad might be home by the time we got back, but when Mum picked us up, she was on her own and I braced myself for bad news.

'What happened, Mum? Where is Dad?' I wasn't sure I wanted to hear the answer.

'He's got to stay in jail for a while longer.' She was careful not to overwhelm Roman and me with the awfulness of it all immediately. I think she was trying to come to terms with it herself. I didn't ask how long he would be away, because any amount of time would be too much. I was silent for a while before I asked my standard school pick-up question.

'Oh, OK. What's for tea?'

Dad had been sentenced to twelve years. Of course, the truth is not quite as it appeared in the press or on the internet. He was made out to be a thug and a lunatic, which isn't the case. He got into a fight at a car auction because of a long running grudge and it got out of hand. The family couldn't believe he had been sent down for so long and my young brain couldn't compute that length of time: it just sounded like forever. Dad appealed and they cut his sentence to eleven years, but that didn't seem any shorter to me. I couldn't imagine him not being there for the rest of my childhood and teenage years. How was I going to cope without seeing him every day? I already missed him so much, sometimes it felt like a physical ache.

Dad started his sentence in Strangeways Prison, which was a tough place to be. Mum visited him a couple of times a week and we would go with her every Saturday. When I think about it, it was a crazy experience, but as a kid you have a very different response from the one I would have now if I stepped inside a prison. All I really focused on was seeing my dad – that was all I cared about, and I didn't take much notice of who or what was around me.

We had to arrive at the prison about forty-five minutes before our allotted visiting time and go to a separate building to sign in. From there we were walked to the jail and would endure a series of body searches with our belongings in a tray, just like security at airports. We went through several gates and at each section a big shutter came down and we had more checks before we were allowed to proceed. At the end, we were ushered through a door into a massive hall where all the prisoners sat waiting for their visitors.

The first time I saw Dad there was so much to take in. I couldn't believe he was standing in front of me, and we were allowed to hug and kiss him before we sat down. We only had an hour, so we told him what we had been up to. There was a shop behind a little hatch where you could buy sandwiches, chocolate and drinks. Roman and I always got something to eat, and while Mum and Dad chatted about lawyers and legal plans, we would flick the lid of a drinks bottle to each other. Dad was on one side of the table and we were on the other, and we weren't allowed to reach over. We knew we had to be well-behaved or else. I don't know what the else was, but the prison guards didn't look like fun. The hour was up all too fast and we hugged and kissed goodbye until the next week. In between visits, Dad was allowed to call once a day.

Dad was, and still is, the joker of our family. He is great company, a real laugh and an off-the-cuff sort of man who would surprise us at the most unexpected moments. I loved his spontaneity: we could get up for breakfast and he would change the course of the day's events with the promise of a road trip to Wales when he got home from work. Or we might be sitting around the table having tea and he would come in and announce that we needed to be up bright and early the following morning for a five-hour drive because we were taking the caravan to Cornwall. Nana and Grandad would usually join us too. I couldn't wait for these last-minute holidays: they were so exciting, and we never knew where we would end up. Mum was always well up for it too, and would go along with his madcap arrangements as long as it fitted into the school schedule or was at a time when we wouldn't be missed for a day or two. She understood the education system better than Dad, and didn't agree to us bunking off whenever he fancied a minibreak.

All of a sudden, this life was over. The realisation of what Dad's prison sentence meant, not just to him but to us too, took a while to sink in, and when it did, I felt a sadness I had not experienced in my young life. I know a lot of children deal with their parents divorcing and not being able to see their dads every day, but many can still meet up, visit at the weekend or pick up the phone. We couldn't, and that came to be one of the hardest things about that time. There were days when I was very aware of his absence and what he and we were missing out on. It meant that I looked forward to the times I did see him or speak to him, and I didn't take them for granted. It wasn't in great circumstances or against the best backdrop, but the way I felt on the morning of a prison visit, knowing we would spend an hour with him, or when he was on day release and came home to hang out with us, made my heart burst with pleasure, and that was the silver lining of a very dark cloud: it made me appreciate the time we had together.

Before Dad went to prison, he would take us to the gym at his brother Peter's holiday home park in Warrington where Tyson and my cousin Hughie trained, so we were all there together. Tyson was doing brilliantly, and Hughie was an amazing boxer too who had won the World Amateur Championships and was turning professional. Without Dad, my uncle Peter stepped in and took on Tyson's training as well as working with Roman and me. Mum dropped us off there after school and we would work out for a couple of hours. She hung around and waited for us, popping into Makro, the wholesale supermarket, to pass the time. I thank her for near enough everything in my life because she would take me to every single training session when Dad was in jail and I was too young to get the bus. She made sure that whatever time it was, she got me there. Without her support, I couldn't have done it. I don't think she realised this was going to be my career, or how seriously I wanted to take it: she was just ferrying her son to his hobby, something he enjoyed doing. But I was beginning to wonder if this was my destiny, particularly as my education was in freefall.

Secondary school was a disaster for me. I am not going to use the excuse that I couldn't focus due to my dad being in jail, because I don't think it would have made any difference if he hadn't been; in fact, it may have made things worse, as he would have encouraged me to leave. In my first year there I really tried tackling all the subjects, but it was a big step up from primary school and I quickly began to struggle. I wasn't academic. I was OK at English and science but rubbish at maths. Maths and I never got on. I couldn't understand algebra; it was like someone was speaking French to me, which I was also not good at, although I did make a valiant effort to understand mathematics. I stayed behind for extra lessons, but it just didn't click. Everyone else seemed to be progressing much faster than me, and it seemed like it came naturally to others, whereas I just couldn't keep up. Easily distracted, I became a bit of a Jack the Lad, and it would annoy the teachers. I don't think they liked me very much, although I was never rude or disrespectful (at least I hope I wasn't, because that's not how I was brought up) but I wasn't a model student. My saving grace and favourite subject at secondary school was PE, and it was the only thing I excelled in.

This may sound like a cop out, but I just knew I wouldn't need to be academic. I could read and write to a good level and count money, so I figured that was all that was required for what I wanted to do. By the second year I was giving up on education and focusing on my life outside school, which was rugby and boxing. Parents' evenings were not fun. There was a lot of, 'if Tommy spent less time staring out of the window or rolling around on the ground wrestling people and more time focusing on his work in class . . .' Mum would despair of me.

'What's going on, Tommy? Why don't you listen in class? What are you playing at?' she would ask, exasperated.

'I am trying!' I would say, and then make lots of things up to save my own sorry arse. Sometimes Nana would be there too because Dad was in prison, although he wouldn't have attended even if he had been around. No threats, encouragement, bribery or guilt-tripping worked on me: I was certain I didn't need a traditional education. I was so headstrong; you couldn't tell me anything. I also felt like the school system had given up on me first, but I didn't know how to verbalise that or ask for help, particularly as I had my eyes on a different prize.

As my fixation with boxing grew, I had to make a difficult decision. Rugby was going well for Roman and me: we were pretty good. I scored seven or eight tries in one game, and the coach for the year above asked me if I would play for them too. We got a few trials for Salford City Reds, which was a big deal and showed we had both got to a serious standard, but I began to fall out of love with it. I had thought that rugby would give me a career and I needed to focus on it and stick to boxing in my spare time, but then I found that boxing was taking over. I gave up rugby when I was fourteen to fully concentrate on boxing. If I hadn't come from a fighting family, maybe I would have pursued rugby. Who knows?

I decided to put all my energy into boxing, much to my teachers' frustrations.

'You need a plan B, Tommy, if the boxing doesn't work out,' they would say. 'What will you have to fall back on? I bet loads of kids here want to be footballers, but how many actually make it?' It fell on deaf ears.

Of course, I understand why they said this. They were hoping there was still time to get me to focus on my studies and scrape through with a handful of exam qualifications, but it was way too late and nothing they said made the slightest bit of difference to me.

'Well, guess what, if it doesn't work out, I will cross that bridge when I come to it,' I would respond, and hope I didn't sound too rude.

If I had a backup plan, then that would take my mind off what I needed to do and I was not prepared to take that risk because my dream required a hundred per cent of me, otherwise I was not going to make it. I didn't listen to the teachers or my mum. There was nothing else at that school for me, but it was going to take time and ingenuity to extricate myself from it. I carried the conviction and passion that I was going to be a fighter. I could have wasted my time on an alternative 'just in case' scenario, but not having one made me hungrier. Not one teacher spoke to me positively about my dreams. They didn't take time to get to know me or see how well I was doing in the boxing gym, but maybe that was because by then I was just a troublemaker to them: a lost cause who refused to toe the line. I can see how difficult it was for them.

It didn't help that I got suspended for a few days. Annoyingly, it was in my favourite subject, PE, playing table tennis. Grandad had taught me well and I was enjoying the game until my opponent accused me of cheating and hurled the paddle at me. I saw red, went over to him and threw a couple of fists his way.

'Ah, well done, Son, it will be all right, don't worry about it,' my dad said when I told him I had been in a fight with someone when we were on our next prison visit. Mum went mad at him.

'What are you telling him that for?' she said. 'He will only go and do it again!' I didn't though. I always knew in any school predicament that Dad would just find it funny, while Mum would give me hell for it. Nothing is as it was when my dad was a child. Travellers usually remain in education these days, but back then it was primary school only and then the girls would stay at home with their mothers to help with chores and look after younger siblings while the boys would go with their fathers to learn a trade.

That was what I wanted to do: join the family trade of boxing and be in the gym full time with my brothers and cousins.

Roman and I trained together, and while I wanted to step into the ring, he was doing it for exercise, although that changed a few years ago when he decided to focus on boxing and turned professional. He and I did everything together, always playing football and rugby, wrestling and throwing shots at each other. At the gym we met up with the rest of our brothers and we went to as many of Tyson's events as possible. He was already doing very well, with big wins and several belts to his name, and he was world ranked. I trained alongside him as he got ready for various fights and he was so helpful, even when he was in the zone for the next big bout. There was no bullying among any of us; we were friends as much as we were family. I have so many brilliant memories of those years and we continue to create more as I am still close to all my brothers now.

At the start, when Tyson was boxing, I would never mention it at primary school and people didn't put two and two together even though our surname is quite unusual. Nobody knew he was my brother, and it wasn't important to me to talk about it. It wasn't discovered until Dad went to prison. By then Tyson was quite famous, so the headlines were full of things like

'Fury's father jailed for twelve years', but I tried not to take any notice of them. I went into school one day and there was a rumour that I was related to Tyson. One of the kids asked me if it was true. I said yes. And then a teacher asked me if my dad was around, and I said he wasn't at the moment, which was probably code for 'he's in the nick'. Suddenly, when people realised the connection between me and Tyson, more kids wanted to chat to me and be friends. I wasn't interested; I had never sought to be popular and I wasn't a boaster. I certainly wouldn't have used Tyson to get attention. I was proud of him, but his achievements were his and not for me to brag about. I still feel the same way.

When the kids knew I was the brother of the Gypsy King and the son of a Gypsy, there was also some name-calling. Kids can be cruel, and they can find a nasty nickname for someone whether it's about the colour of their skin, their sexuality or their beliefs. I got 'gypo' or 'pikey' for a while, but it didn't last long because I was broad and big and could always hold my own. I don't think anyone wanted to mess with me, so I didn't get bullied about my heritage. If others had something to say about it, then they said it behind my back for fear I may practise my sparring combinations on them!

From thirteen I was training harder than a professional. I was up at 4 a.m. six days a week to go out running. I had laid my kit and trainers out the night before including a hoodie and coat because it was freezing at that time in the morning. I silently slipped out through the front door, popped my headphones in and was off, pounding the streets for five miles or so. When I got back, I went into the garage at the side of the house, spent an hour pummelling Dad's boxing bag, followed by some weights I could barely lift, and finished the session with a few press-ups and sit-ups. Back in the house, I couldn't risk showering because it would wake everyone, so I dried myself off with a towel and got back into bed. Gross, I know, but I slept until my alarm went off at 8 a.m., then jumped in the shower before heading to school. That was my routine for over two years, and I rarely missed a morning.

As well as my brother Tyson, his namesake, Mike Tyson, was a massive inspiration to me. He was the fighter that I wanted to be like: the wrecking ball. I used to watch Mike on YouTube and he said he got up at 4 a.m. to run in the pitch dark because he felt like it gave him a little edge on his competitors, who would still be fast asleep. I will never forget that. I knew that was what I needed to do to separate myself from the rest. Every kid in the country could go training at set times to the gym, but I knew that most teenagers would not be getting up at that time and running before dawn. This attitude would put me physically and mentally above the rest. I felt like Rocky Balboa when I left the house and at first, I would swallow a raw egg like he did, but pretty quickly I realised that this was what was giving me a stitch ten minutes into my run. Sometimes what works in movies does not work in real life. Let that be a lesson to us all.

It was hard to be without Dad over those years. Particularly as boxing was becoming a bigger deal in my life and many young boxers would have their dads with them during training and at the ringside. I felt lonely without my own dad by my side, and it did make me grow up faster – there's no doubt about that. But as Tyson used to say, there was no point crying over spilled milk. That has now become one of our family mottos. If I had decided not to start training until Dad got out, it would have been the wrong mindset to have and I wouldn't have got anywhere. I had to take my ambition into my own hands and make it my mission to continue, whether Dad was there or not.

Mum took a similar attitude. Her priority was to protect us and keep everything on an even keel, but she knew she couldn't sit at home all day waiting around for Dad to be released, so she enrolled at the University of Salford on a three-year degree course in podiatry. She dropped Roman and me at school every morning, drove to the university for lectures and studied for six hours before picking us up on the way home. Then she would put her books to one side and cook our tea. She could have nose-dived or taken to her bed, but she didn't. She could have said she had her hands full, solo parenting two busy, sporty boys but she didn't. She could have missed prison visits because she had too much on, but she didn't. She held it all together, kept the show on the road and, other than Dad not being there, nothing changed for us. She was the best mum in the world to us, looked out for Dad and used the time we were at school wisely. You wouldn't have known what she was going through as she kept her emotions in check when we were around; we still had a lot of fun as a family and Grandad kindly paid for us all to go on holiday. Those years were such a mix of awful and great, but none of us sat around moping – life continued. Mum graduated, in cap and gown, just before Dad was released, and we were all so proud of what she had achieved.

While Dad was in prison, Nana (my mum's mum) would write to him near enough every day for five years. We still have all the letters in a box at home. She is the only woman on earth who can give my dad a run for his money, and she laughs at all his chest-beating, name-calling boxing behaviour at press conferences and in the ring. Whenever he is wrong, she is the first to inform him that he has screwed up;

she has no problem telling him off and he respects that. She is formidable! Nana is always on the go and can't keep still; she loves cleaning everyone's houses, gardening and feeding the birds. She is feisty for all the right reasons and a large presence; you can't miss her in the room. I think that's why she and Dad get on so well: they are both loud and outgoing. It's funny to watch the two of them together. They may have a big row, but the following morning she will come round and drop off a bunch of bananas for him as a sort of peace offering because she knows he loves them. Then he will call her.

'Thanks for them bananas, Barbara, appreciate it, see you in a bit,' he will say.

Our family are very good at saying 'it's all water under the bridge' – another oft-repeated phrase – and if there are cross words or a fall out, it is quickly resolved.

Dad moved from Strangeways to Buckley Hall Prison in Rochdale, then to Thorn Cross Prison in Warrington, which was when he was allowed out for home visits. We would pick him up on Saturday morning and drop him back on Sunday night. He had to stay close to home but we could go out for a walk, get some food and do a bit of training on the pads. It was such a relief to have him around again, and things began to return to normal.

One weekend, I was invited to a sparring session at my uncle's gym in Warrington. There were a load of lads getting together, it was a bit of an event, and my uncle thought I might enjoy it. I was about thirteen and my interest in boxing was growing. I so clearly remember opening the door to the gym to be faced with a big group of people, including every type of boxer you could imagine – from the slight featherweights to the bruising heavies and everything in between. There were a few good boxing coaches and industry scouts there too, sniffing around for a promising newcomer. Fighters were matched up for sparring rounds and I was the last up. I got into the ring and sparred with another travelling lad who may have had five or six fights to his name by this point – he was certainly much more experienced than I was. I let rip, and nobody expected it. I had always been one of a gang of brothers who had hung out at the gym, trained and had a go at the bags and now there I was, holding my own, looking like I knew what I was doing. I could tell everyone had taken notice.

'Where did that come from?' someone asked me afterwards. 'Have you ever had a fight?'

'No,' I said, glad that I had caused a reaction, 'not yet.' I could feel my confidence growing with every look in my direction and it fuelled my ambition. That was when word started to get out about me. For the first time, I thought maybe Tyson wasn't going to be the only champion in the family.

I had spent a couple of years committed to early morning training and evenings spent in the Warrington gym with my brothers and cousins, and I was sure I had it in me to go to the next level. I told my uncle I wanted to step into the ring. I knew I was ready for my first fight, and he agreed. He said he knew the trainer for me, so on Tuesday and Thursday nights I was coached by Tommy Battle and sparred with the boys at his club, Metro ABC Gym in Bolton. Tommy could only get me a fight if he thought I was ready, so I waited impatiently for the nod. Within a week of being there I was sparring with his best boys because I had been used to training with Tyson and Hughie. Tyson taught me stuff in the gym that I still use to this day, and he has always kept a close eye on me, particularly in those years when our dad couldn't.

When Tommy said it was time for me to get in the ring, I nearly exploded with excitement and antici-pation, and then winning my first amateur fight (as I described at the beginning of this book) was not only a big turning point for me, but also a moment when everyone else took note of how much I wanted it. My brutal training routine and dedication to sport was not normal behaviour for the average teenager, and I had proved my commitment to my future career. Of course, the first win could have been a fluke, but I was eager to prove it wasn't. The only thing that was now holding me back was the fact I was still at school.

I had a burning desire to succeed, and I knew it was different because with however many hundreds of kids in that school, there was not one training like me. All the kids who wanted to be footballers or athletes or sports people might train on a Tuesday and Thursday and play a match on Sunday, but I was up every morning and out each night, running, training and taking knocks off heavyweights. I knew what I wanted to do and where I wanted to go and most importantly, I knew what it took to get there. What was inside me separated me from the rest and I was determined to make something of myself.

After my second amateur fight, school was over for me. I knew boxing was my future and I took my two wins as a sign. It was pointless to go through the motions at school and pretend for any longer, and I knew I had little hope of passing my exams. It all seemed like a massive waste of my time, and it was also unfair on the teachers who were still pushing me to succeed. I would drag myself there every day and spend the lessons upset and frustrated. It didn't take long for the school to notice the energy I was giving off had reached an all-time low, and they asked for a meeting with me and Mum.

I wasn't worried by this; in fact, I felt the exact opposite. This was my one chance, my only opportunity to convince them all that there could be another way. I desperately wanted Mum and the school to understand how I felt and why I wanted to leave. My educational years had been torturous, so it wasn't going to come as a shock to anyone, but I wanted to prove that I wasn't bailing because I wanted to sit on my arse at home all day. Quite the opposite. I had stuff to do. I had a dream to pursue, and I couldn't waste a single minute.

Mum came in and we sat down with my head of year and the deputy head of the school. I didn't beat around the bush – I told it how it was.

'You guys know I am not academic, and I have no interest in any of the subjects. I don't want to be here. I have something I want to chase, something that is really important to me, and I won't get it being here.' I wasn't just saying this to shut them up; this was my plan. If I couldn't make it as a boxer, then something else would come up. The important thing was not to entertain any doubt right now, because if I questioned myself for one moment they might spot a chink in my armour, and all would be lost. I can still remember that feeling now, like putting all your chips on black, holding your breath and watching the roulette wheel spin.

They asked me questions about my boxing routine and how often I trained. When I told them I got up at 4 a.m. every morning and went to training sessions at the gym after school every evening, I could see their attitude shift. They knew I was serious. We came to an agreement. The deal was that I could be absent from school for training, as long as I still sat the exams, so that is what I did. I could come and go as much as my gym schedule allowed, and with this decision came an overriding sense of utter relief.

I know this plan may sound risky to you, but leaving education early is part of the Traveller culture so it didn't feel unusual to me to be out at fifteen, and I think the school took that into consideration too. That said, I would not encourage anyone to do what I did. I think my situation was unique. I can say this now as a father who would not allow his daughter to do the same unless she had a cast-iron reason! I sincerely hope she has a better school experience than I did and that she will speak up to Molly and me and to her teachers if she is struggling with something. I should have done that when I started at secondary school, rather than drown in confusion.

That final year of school was much easier, and I was happier too. Now that everyone knew what I was going on to do, that I was just there to sit the exams and not forced to attend lessons, it took a huge weight off my shoulders. I was grateful to be listened to and for my views to be respected. It was also important to me that people didn't think it was about hating school because, although I did, that wasn't my reason for leaving. I had a vision and every second was going to count. My plan was to work harder than I ever would have at school.

I ended up getting a couple of GCSEs – PE and RE, I think – but I definitely didn't leave school with anything worth talking about. Even when school was no longer a thing and all the kids in my year had left, I never worried about my lack of results. After their exams, Kyle and the rest of my mates went to Eccles College, which was about half a mile from me. On their first morning there they called me as they were walking past my house and asked me what I was doing and if I wanted to walk to college with them. I had been up early for a five-mile run followed by a training session with weights and had just finished breakfast, so I joined them. It was a chance to catch up with what they had been up to. Not one of them questioned why I wasn't going to college; they had known my plan for a couple of years and completely accepted it. Their journey was not mine. When we got to the gates, everyone walked in and I was left on my own, so I turned around and came home again, ready for a midday work-out session and then an evening in the gym. I knew that nothing would have made me walk into that college, and it never crossed my mind that I might have made the wrong decision. I wasn't hanging around, staying in bed and playing computer games, with no idea of what to do next. I was a workhorse on my own type of apprenticeship – in a boxing gym. I never doubted myself, because I was convinced things would work out for me and, if they didn't, I would have no regrets. It seems mad to think this was less than ten years ago because in many ways I feel a whole lifetime has passed.

Dad missed a lot while he was inside: as well as four years of his boys' lives, he also lost two of his brothers during this time, both in their early fifties. He had three brothers – Peter, Huey and Jimmy. Jimmy died of a heart attack, but Huey's story is particularly tragic as he had gone into hospital with a broken ankle. It was put in a cast, and he went home, but complained of it being too tight, so a few days later he went back in to get it sorted. By then he had got a blood clot and it travelled to his heart, killing him. This was devastating for Dad, and tragic for Grandma, who outlived two of her sons and died a few years later. I can't imagine losing one of my siblings and having to cope with the shape of our family shifting for ever.

When Dad went to prison, I wanted to be a rugby player, and when he came out, I was a boxer. When he went to prison, I was a boy, and when he came out, I was a man.

3

Amateur Hour

*We have all lost fights in the past, it comes
with the territory. Accept it and move on.
It's how you get up and get back out there
that counts.*

I left school at fifteen (if we ignore the small matter
of still needing to take a handful of GCSEs) and I
had already made my debut in the amateur fighting
world. My first fight had created a bit of hype, people
were taking interest in me, and my training went up
a notch. Working with Tommy Battle was unbelievable – I loved training with him because he was so
emotionally invested. If you weren't doing well in a
fight, he would throw everything and the kitchen sink

at you – it was hilarious. He was lovely, very funny and completely down to earth, and we had a great relationship. When I went to him at Metro ABC in Bolton, I was inexperienced but he took my raw talent and persevered, so when he saw me in the ring in my first fight, he was so proud of me. In the short time I had been working with him I had come a long way.

After the first fight I knew this was what I wanted to do for the rest of my life. Whatever that feeling was, I wanted it again and again. I asked Tommy when he could get me out there and so the next fight was organised for a couple of months later. It was even better than the first one. The fight was held at a leisure centre in Heywood, and I was lined up to box Nico Carlton, who came from a famous gym in Manchester, the Collyhurst and Moston Boxing Club. Lots of great boxers had come out of it. I remember everyone had been talking about Nico. He had only fought once before and knocked his opponent clean out, so it was a big test for me. It didn't help that he was already 6' 2" at fifteen and I was about 5' 10".

On the night I had the usual mix of nerves, anticipation and ambition, but this time around the little voice inside my head wondered if my previous win had been a fluke. What if that was as good as it got and it was downhill from now? I was also unwell with a flu bug and had a hacking cough, so I did not know how much stamina I would have. I could feel all the usual pressure with the addition of now having something to live up to.

This time I had a few more supporters. Hughie, Roman and my uncle were there along with a few of my friends, and Tommy was in my corner. It was a much tougher test than the first fight and we had a really good tear up. I think all that got me through was the desire to win and the courage I felt when I faced my opponent. When I got into the ring something shifted and I wanted that feeling of triumph again; nobody was going to take it away from me, so I let my punches go and landed my shots. I caught Nico's nose and a lot of blood splattered over my shorts and flecked the canvas. It was an impressive win and another unanimous decision. The show was going on and I was getting better.

As part of my new independence from school, I started to get the bus to training. My uncle had bought a building on Halliwell Road in Bolton and turned it into the Team Fury gym. The Warrington gym had a ring and weights, but nothing compared to the purpose-built Bolton place which was spread out on three levels. On the ground floor was the weight-training room, the next floor up was the boxing gym and the third floor had a kitchen and bedrooms where we could stay for training camps. The facilities were so much better, so everyone moved there to continue training, which is why I went, even though the journey was laborious and sapped the lifeblood from me. I still get flashbacks to that time and can be minding my own business driving around town and spot a bus stop or a road that was a big part of my life back then. I can see the teenage me trudging down the road with a gym bag slung over my shoulder, or loitering impatiently for a bus.

I had to set off from home at 7 a.m., walk forty-five minutes to the bus stop, wait however long and then get on the bus to Bolton, which took over an hour because it pulled up at every stop, which I never failed to find infuriating. Once I got off, I still had to walk for another fifty minutes to the gym. I did this five days a week, often without enough money for the whole journey, so I would try and jump on the bus avoiding paying, get chucked off and then get on the next one. Once, I was thrown off because I was five pence short. But I would always find my way there; I didn't let anything stop me. By the time I arrived at the gym, three hours after I had left home, lugging a heavy bag on my shoulder, I had a full sweat on. I trained for a couple of hours and then had to do the same journey in reverse. It was like working an eight-hour day. Looking back on it, I was just a kid, and yet I didn't miss a single session, travelling in all weather conditions and waiting at the bus stop in the rain, wind and snow. It was brutal, but it was that or give up on my dream, so I knew I had to do it. I think I am an example of what you can achieve with drive and purpose, which doesn't mean you don't need talent, but without the other two, you will find it harder to get out of bed in the morning. I know it wasn't my ability that kept me going; it was the mental commitment that saw me standing at that bus stop.

My third fight was in Club 147, the snooker hall and sports venue in Salford. It was a very small arena and everyone was squashed around the ring together which seemed to create a more hostile environment. The audience was breathing down my neck. It was a tough fight and the first time that I didn't get it all my own way. My opponent came out gunning for me, rocking and rolling, throwing big swings. I was in no doubt that he wanted to win, and I felt our energy for glory was matched. The first round was mine. In the second round, I hit him with three or four right hands on the bounce. I felt like I was in the middle of one of the *Rocky* films. The referee jumped in to give him a standing eight count before he staggered upright. I was well in control, but the last round was very scrappy as my opponent came back out with a lot of aggression and upped the tempo. It was my first experience of this, and I learned a lot in those final few minutes. I threw some more shots and won by unanimous decision again. That was three out of three. I knew I was getting better with each fight and, now my name was out there, even sparring partners had heard about me before they met me.

By this point, more was changing in my boxing life because Dad had been released from prison. While we were all thrilled to have him back, I was doubly grateful that he was joining me at this stage of my boxing journey. It was almost like he hadn't been away. He didn't talk much about his experience inside other than to say it was awful, but it was done, he had served his time and we all needed to move on from it, so that's what we did. It wasn't a taboo subject, but none of us wanted to dwell on what had been. Even now, maybe if we are on a long drive somewhere, I might ask him the odd question about that time, what it was like and how he felt, and he will talk a little bit about it, but we don't have big discussions. We picked up from where we left off and he stepped back into his role as trainer for me and my brothers.

I was rattling through my fights and won the fourth with ease. Boxing on the amateur circuit was proving to be an invaluable start, and I look back on it with a lot of affection because it prepared me well. It got me used to walking in the ring, being in front of the crowd and facing fighting styles I hadn't faced before.

I don't like to show off, but everything was going brilliantly at this point. The only thing I hadn't experienced was losing. Yet. You know what's coming.

I was in Bolton for my fifth fight, two minutes from where I trained, and this was a rematch with the opponent from my third fight. I wasn't too concerned because I had beaten him the first time, although I knew that meant he would have something to prove. It was a close fight and went almost the same way as the first time around, just without the standing count, but I lost on a split decision. It could have gone either way. I was gutted. It was the hardest pill to swallow because I knew I didn't lose the fight and everyone there, including my dad and a couple of trainers, seemed to agree. Listen, I am a fair guy and I can also be my own harshest critic. If I thought I had lost I would say so, but I truly believed I had won the fight and yet didn't get the decision. I was still just a kid and I cried on the way out and on the way home – and when I got into bed I sobbed. I had not yet learned how to handle this type of emotion, and I felt like I had failed everyone. My world came crashing down. I didn't want to get out from under the duvet and I even took a week off from the gym, which was unheard of for me.

In amateur boxing, judges are always under scrutiny for making the wrong call and most of them haven't been in the ring themselves. Questionable decisions are a regular occurrence. I knew they happened, I just didn't think it would happen to me – but it did, and what was important was how I dealt with it. I knew I couldn't let this situation drag me down, so I did what I always did and still do – the only answer I have: I went to the gym.

'Good to see you here.' Tyson slapped me affectionately on the back. He was there training.

'Took the loss hard,' I said, which was a bit of an understatement.

'We've all been there. Me. Hughie. Every boxer I know. We have all lost fights in the past, it comes with the territory. Accept it and move on. It's how you get up and get back out there that counts.' Tyson always knew what to say in these situations. He had a list of great affirmations that never failed to make me feel better.

'Yep, it's all character building,' I admitted reluctantly. 'We go again.'

'That's the spirit!' Tyson wandered off and I went a few rounds with the punchbag. It was a great lesson, which was handy because what I would be facing in the future would turn out to prove much harder to bounce back from.

I entered the England Novice Championships, which was for boxers who have fought fewer than ten fights. It was a competition that my brothers Tyson and my cousin Hughie had won in the past, so yet again I was following in their footsteps – with the added stress of upholding the family's winning streak. Plus, if I triumphed, it would be my first medal and further recognition of what I could do. I won the first and second rounds, before getting a bye to the final because there was nobody else to fight. This was a big moment in my fledgling career.

My opponent in the final was Robert Davis, another Travelling lad from Rotherham in Yorkshire, which is where the fight was held. There was a big buzz of excitement about it because it was billed as a fight between two Traveller families, a real clash of the clans. We were on at the end of the night, and when I got in the ring I could feel the electricity of war in the air. All of Robert's family were there and I had Dad, Roman, Cousin Hughie and Tommy Battle. Robert was bigger and more experienced than me, but my power and determination powered me through.

'I ain't losing! I have not come this far to get beaten,' I said to myself.

In the first round it wasn't going in my direction, and I was getting hit with the jab and tangled up. As the bell went, I went back to my corner and Tommy told me Robert was having his way with me and the judge would be scoring in his favour.

'You need to pick it up!' Tommy urged. That was

all I needed to hear. I came out in the second round like a man possessed. As soon as the bell rang, I went straight into the middle of the ring and I was ducking and diving, throwing everything with bad intentions, and the hits started to land. After I nailed him with a few punches he went on the back foot, and I continued to press him. In the third round, I was hitting him with some big clean shots. When they announced me the winner, I felt a wave of emotion unlike anything I had experienced before. I was the English Under Ten Fights champion.

From there I went straight into the nationals and my ninth fight was against a massive 6' 8" guy for the North West England title, which I won. In the next round, I fought in Liverpool and then went through to the final. I was boxing at heavyweight in the amateurs and there weren't many of us. In the final I was against a boxer who had thirty-six fights to his name, and I lost on a split decision. It was a hard defeat, but I didn't take it too much to heart. I knew that wouldn't get me anywhere and besides, I reminded myself that I had got to the final with only ten fights under my belt, and I was up against someone much more experienced than me. With each fight, I wasn't just gaining skills, I was also growing in maturity and better able to handle my emotions.

My amateur career lasted eighteen months with no

senior bouts. The final fight was in Selby, against an opponent who was on his home turf for the Yorkshire title and I beat him quite convincingly. By this point, I was well known on the amateur circuit. Out of my twelve fights, I had ten wins and two losses. Over two thirds of amateur boxers turn professional after sixty to eighty bouts. Tyson did it after thirty-four. But Roman went professional without any amateur experience, which is not unheard of either. I felt like I had gained everything I needed to, and I was raring to move on. When I think about it now, it feels like a blur, but at the time it felt like forever. Dad and I agreed that the twelfth fight would be my last as an amateur boxer. I was done with training my guts out and doing everything right for little reward. Boxing is a tough sport, and if it was going to be my career then I needed to start making some money to support myself. I had to take my dream to the next level.

Around this time, one of my biggest heroes, the American boxer and activist Muhammad Ali died. I felt incredibly sad. I didn't know the man, I had never met him – I only knew him from old fighting footage and interviews – but he felt like a friend. The world had lost a legend. I trawled the internet and watched lots of his fights again, hoping I could pick up a few pointers and learn from the greatest. Many years later, when I was in Las Vegas training for a fight, I met his grandson, Nico Ali Walsh, a professional boxer around the same age as me, who fights uncannily like his grandfather. We met in the gym and sparred together. Randomly, it was also Halloween and we discussed our shared love of the event, so he invited me to his house, opening the door to a few trick or treaters before we went out in fancy dress. He was dressed as Pennywise, the clown from *It*, and I was Michael Myers (obviously), and we walked around the streets which were packed with people, it was like going to a football game. It was such a brilliant atmosphere. Americans are so good at Halloween, but I think we are embracing it more in the UK now too.

So, back to me being seventeen, and there was change in the air. I loved training with my family, but both Tyson and Hughie were doing really well and were often away for training camps and fights which meant it was a bit lonely at the Bolton gym. I talked to Dad about it. He had been inside with the ex-boxer, Pat Barrett, who had been British, Commonwealth and European champion, and ran Collyhurst and Moston Boxing Gym, and he put in a good word for me to him. I ended up training with Pat for over a year. During this time, I even tried my hand at commentating for a boxing show that one of my stable-mates and spar partners was fighting in. I went down to support, and they asked me to commentate.

I was happy to do so, because it got me closer to the action, but it was also a good experience. I did wonder if it was something I could do again, once my boxing career was behind me.

The gym was the other side of Manchester, which created a new type of travel nightmare. It used to take me all morning to get there, and I promise you I am not exaggerating. I had to be at the bus stop outside my house for 6 a.m. to get the bus to the train station. As before, I didn't always have the money for a ticket, so I would find ways to sneak on to public transport. I took the train from Eccles to Manchester and walked twenty minutes to a different bus stop to get the number 81 bus. I could easily wait forty minutes and when I saw the bus coming towards me, the feeling of relief was physical. The bus took me from Manchester city centre to Moston, which in a car would probably be a fifteen-minute journey, but by bus it was close to an hour. And I still wasn't there when I got off the bus because I had another mile to walk to the gym. By the time I was ready to spar, I was exhausted from the early start and travel. After training I would wait for the bus to take me back into the city, walk to the train station, get the train back to Eccles, wait for another bus. There were times, making this return journey every day on repeat, when I thought, I can't do this anymore, it's killing me. I was leaving the house at

6 a.m. and wasn't getting home until almost twelve hours later – and only two hours of that was training. It was verging on madness.

Once, Dad dropped me at the boxing gym because he was going that way. This was rare, and I was so pleased because it meant I had a few extra hours in bed, and I arrived at the gym fresh and ready for action. I trained for ages, it felt great, and after the session I grabbed my gym bag and walked out onto the street when it hit me. I didn't have anything on me: no money, no phone, no bus pass, no coat, and this meant there was no way of getting home. Being given a lift made me forget everything, it had taken the weight off my shoulders, and I had jumped into the car without a single thought about my return. I was so cross with myself. I tried sneaking onto the bus, but the driver knew me and wouldn't listen to my explanations. I walked all the way home from Moston in the torrential rain in just a jumper, weighed down by a heavy gym bag. It took me almost five hours. That was a very low moment. When I got home, I went straight to bed, and I can tell you, I never made that mistake again.

I think the lengthy and tedious travel prepared me mentally. At all times of the year, in blizzards, hailstones, snow, freezing conditions and heatwaves, I would be stood at the bus stop after a session, sweating, hands shaking, a black eye and a busted face, holding a blood-soaked tissue to my nose. I often looked an absolute state, so God knows what other passengers thought, I can't blame them for giving me a wide berth. I think about that time now and how it equipped me for what was to come. Every day was like being in a fight for my right to be at that gym before I'd even done a minute's training. All the trains, buses, pavement-pounding, fare-dodging, stress and time spent waiting made me feel like I had really earned my place.

In 2018, Tyson was preparing for his big comeback after his retirement and publicly documented struggles with alcohol, drugs and mental health issues. He was training at world champion boxer Ricky Hatton's gym in Hyde with our dad. I talked to Dad and told him the travelling to Moston and back was really getting me down.

'Dad, it's killing me to get there and yous are all together at another gym, training under one roof. Can I come and join you?' I asked. He said I could, and managed to get me a trial with Ricky. I had a sparring session in front of him; luckily, he liked what he saw and invited me to come to the gym. I trained there with Tyson, Dad, my uncle and the rest of my brothers and I felt a lot better in myself. OK, so I still had the effort of getting the train and bus there, but it was much closer and when I arrived, I was surrounded by familiar faces. Tyson would watch me spar and I was training like a professional. I was in my element and really came on there. It was my time.

4

Turning TNT

From a fifteen-year-old amateur swinging through his first fight, to four years later as a professional at the Manchester Arena in front of thousands of people and screened live to however many more, how did I get here?

I was nineteen years old when I made my professional boxing debut. As you've seen already, I was not your typical teenager.

I had been spending all my time in the gym, so I didn't have the sort of life you would expect for a young lad. I may have gone out with my mates on special occasions, but boxing came first and, if I did go out, I would always be back on the road, out running by 6 a.m. the following morning. I never took a day off. I did date for a while, but drinking, parties and girlfriends took a back seat. All my attention was on my dream and as soon as I knew I was turning professional, it made it even easier to focus. There was no time for fun. Yet I don't feel that I missed out, even though I didn't do what my friends were doing. I saw them having a good time, but I was so certain of my path, I knew living it up wouldn't get me anywhere and that wasn't the right life for me at that time. I thought I would hold back and when I got to where I wanted to be, things could be different. Tyson always says if you want something, you must make sacrifices, and that's what I did.

The other issue around going out was that I wasn't earning anything, so I didn't have any money to pay for rounds of drinks, entry into clubs or new clothes to dress up in. Luckily, I wasn't interested in fashion. There was no chance of a part-time job because of my training schedule and I didn't care about money, as long as I had a roof over my head and food to eat, which I did, all thanks to my parents. I wanted to train and fight and there was nothing else I needed money for – that was until the lads organised a holiday to Zante in Greece when I was eighteen. This came up prior to my first professional fight and I was desperate for a break in my year of training. Determined to go, I thought about how to save enough money for the flight and hotel and remembered the times Roman and I would walk around the streets when we were younger, me carrying a spade and him wheeling a lawnmower, knocking on people's doors asking if they had any garden tasks we could help with and charging them a fiver. I managed to scrape just enough money together by taking on odd jobs for people and I think Nana had the neatest-cut hedge on the street. Luckily, the holiday was cheap.

We had an absolute blast in Greece. It was the first holiday I'd taken without my parents, and I had never been on a plane before. The week was hilarious, full of carefree days driving around on quads and jumping in the sea, and nights in the clubs, lining up the shots. I loved every minute, and these memories are some of the best I have with my mates. My friend Chris had the most money out of all of us, so he would get the drinks in, and I would always say, 'I'll pay you back one day, mate.' Just so you know, for the avoidance of doubt, I have paid him back! I am so glad I got the opportunity to go on holiday when I did because these days it is much harder to do anything like that without being recognised, and now I am a father and almost a husband, my priorities have changed.

When I left the amateurs behind, I took a year off from getting in the ring to focus on my training and make sure my style suited the professional game. Other than that week in Zante with my mates, I was spending most of my waking hours at Ricky Hatton's gym, sparring with pro boxers. It was a very different approach from what I was used to. As an amateur I would train for no longer than an hour at a time, at a much higher and quicker tempo because I was preparing for three explosive, sharp rounds of two-minute lengths with only six minutes to win the fight. Out running, I might limit my distance to just a couple of miles but with a load of sprints thrown in. Once in the ring, the gloves were bigger, weighing in at ten ounces, and I wore training wraps and a head guard, which I hated because it felt like I couldn't see the shots coming.

As a professional, I would be fighting for up to twelve three-minute rounds, so the training sessions were longer and harder, to prepare me for this format. When I ran, it was for six, eight or even ten miles at a steady regular pace. In the ring I would be taking my time, warming into the fight, and I'd have half an hour to achieve victory. I could sit down on my punches and really relax into it, which I preferred because I don't like to rush my work. Plus I could now fight with smaller gloves and my hands were securely wrapped, so it was like having fists of rock. I could almost feel my fingers at the end of the gloves.

I was going from a point-scoring exercise where the aim is to touch your opponent as many times as you can, to the serious business of hitting and hurting. It was about doing damage and knocking my opponent out which is, in many ways, a completely different sport. I am not a fast starter, as a rule, so the increased number of rounds gave me more time to settle into the fight; my style was more suited to the professional game.

The other big difference between the two was the mental shift. In professional boxing there is more on the line, more to fight for. While the money was a factor, it wasn't what spurred me on. My main goal was to become world champion, and this mattered to me more than anything else – and definitely more than my social life.

I had to have my professional status approved before I could fight. The British Boxing Board of Control make the decision about whether a fighter is ready to turn professional or not, which usually means them coming to the gym to watch you train and, based on what they see, they can say whether you are ready or not. Luckily for me, they had heard about my amateur wins and that I had reached the final of the nationals in a short space of time, so they knew

I could do it. I went to their HQ for the medical and an interview in front of a panel and they handed me my licence there and then. It was a good feeling and a big tick in the box.

More great news was on the way. Within a few weeks I got a meeting with Frank Warren, the iconic boxing promoter, which was a real coup and exactly what I needed as I turned professional, because he's one of those people who makes stuff happen. One sunny day in October, I drove down to his offices in Hertfordshire with a couple of guys from my gym team, trying to keep my nerves in check. This was just going to be a chat, after all, with no promises or guarantees. But I knew I was lucky to get time with Frank and I didn't want to blow it. I needn't have worried. It was a very relaxed conversation and he asked me lots of questions about my approach as a boxer, how I felt in the ring and if I was enjoying it.

'So, when are you fit to fight?' he asked.

'I am in shape now, because I don't do anything else but train.' Frank was pleased to hear it.

'Perfect, I have got the twenty-second of December free if you are available for that?'

I think my jaw must have dropped wide open. That was the date of the Josh Warrington and Carl Frampton card. It was a big fight with a lot of heat around it and it was happening at Manchester Arena

in a couple of months. I knew all of this already because I'd been hoping to go to it. Josh and Carl were
headlining and here was Frank, offering me the undercard and asking if I was happy to go ahead?! I thought
my professional debut would be in a leisure centre or
an old school gym somewhere in front of four hundred people maximum, but that wasn't Frank's style. I
couldn't believe I had gone from trying to buy a ticket
to go to the fight, to actually boxing on the undercard
in my home city; it was one of my biggest wishes to
box there. It was unknown for a first fight to have that
sort of kudos, yet things were happening and putting
themselves in place. I couldn't really process it.

I took the offer with both hands and thanked Frank
profusely, before heading back to Manchester with a
stop off at Burger King. I know. I just couldn't help
myself. I turned to the guys from my gym team as we
pulled up.

'Should I be eating this if I have only got seven
weeks to get in shape?' I was basically looking for
permission to get a Double Whopper.

'Listen, mate,' one of them said, laughing, 'you have
just been given a fight on one of the biggest cards of
the year, get whatever you want!'

So I did and I felt sick with the amount of food I
ate – I think it was four burgers. I was completely
taking the mickey, but I knew this was the last

opportunity I'd have to treat myself for a couple of months. The following morning, I started training in earnest, as if my life depended on it – because it did.

I was booked to fight Latvian boxer Jevgenijs Andrejevs, who had 130 professional bouts compared to my total of zero. Even though he didn't have a great record, it was unusual for a match to be so uneven. Normally for a first fight you get a journeyman, a fighter who has enough skill to match their opponent, boxes frequently and is not expected to win. Their job is to get in there, get the rounds in and put other boxers through their paces so they easily clock up several fights a week. They may lose the majority of them, but they have put the time in, gained the experience and they are there for the pay cheque. The problem with us Fury boys is that we don't get the journeymen approaching us in this way because whenever anyone hears our last name, all that goes out the window. Every time anyone fights one of us it's about beating us, and we always seem to be faced with an opponent who wants to crush our family.

As well as the punishing training schedule, there were other aspects of the professional life that I had to give some time to. Like choosing my boxing nickname, which would be part of my brand and merchandising if I went on to be successful. Tyson is called 'The Gypsy King', Mike Tyson was known as 'Iron Mike' at one point and Muhammad Ali was simply 'The Greatest'. Who was I going to be? The answer came when I was messing around with friends, and we were all shouting out possible name combinations. Like Tommy 'Gun' Fury. And Tommy 'AK47' Fury. Someone suggested Tommy 'TNT' Fury, and I thought that kind of fitted. I repeated it a few times, decided to give it a go for my first fight and it has stuck ever since. Several people even call me TNT now, rather than Tommy.

The other difference between professional and amateur boxing is the media interest. I took part in my first press conference the month before the fight. I immediately felt confident in the new environment, and I was on peak form, hoping I looked slick in a black leather shearling jacket and white polo neck.

I was introduced as the name of the moment, Tommy 'TNT' Fury, Tyson's younger brother, and asked how I was feeling about my debut.

'I can't wait, it feels like a long time coming. I have been training all year and I'm ready to let my fists do the talking. I am not doing it because of my name. I want to show people what I've really got.' I spoke clearly and calmly. The interviewer could see my dad standing at the back and he asked if I felt the burden of expectation and I answered honestly, about Tyson being Tyson and Hughie being Hughie and how I was going to be me. Of course I was grateful for what I had learned from them, 'but now it is my time. You can't replicate anybody. If I can do half as well as them, then it will be a privilege, but I am looking at myself and my career. I am not going to rush. I am nineteen. I am just going to go in the ring and do my best.' I think – I hope – I came across as composed, articulate and ready for what was ahead. Asked if I would get to LA for Tyson's fight against Deontay Wilder on 1 December, I said I wouldn't, but I would be cheering on from the settee.

The interviewer wanted to know how inspirational it was for me to see my brother come back from a pretty low place after a well-documented battle with addiction and mental illness.

'It's a win it itself. He was twenty-nine stone, rock bottom, you couldn't get any lower, so he has won already. He had two comeback fights, and he is straight in line for the WBC world title. How many fighters do you know who have done this?' I could hear the murmur of agreement around the room. 'If anyone can, it's Tyson. If he is forty per cent the boxer he was in 2015 he will clean up because he has too much skill for anyone. Nearly seven-foot tall, twenty stone and he moves like a featherweight. I haven't seen it before. Muhammad Ali was fifteen stone and 6' 2". Tyson is a giant and moves just like Ali.'

The press conference was coming to an end, with the last couple of questions to go. The interviewer was still on Tyson and he asked how proud I would be if Tyson pulled the fight off. Only one answer to that.

'I couldn't get any prouder. Becoming two times champion of the world, it sounds great, doesn't it?' Then there was finally a question about me and whether I would be nervous on the twenty-second. 'Always, but I have to take it in my stride, this is what I do day in and day out in the gym. It's just a few more eyes on you. I am going to go out there, do what I can do and start the journey off. That's what I am looking forward to.' I thanked everyone for being there and handed the microphone back.

The questions were very Tyson focused, but I understood that. I was his little brother with no professional fights to my name and very little to talk about. Plus, Tyson's fight was much anticipated, huge, and scheduled before mine, so of course I was going to be asked about it. People were intrigued by my rise through the amateur ranks, but it was my brother who everyone was fascinated by. Maybe some of them expected me to fail, or hoped I would, and I am sure many thought that there was only room for one champion in the family. After all, lightning doesn't strike in the same place twice.

Fast forward to fight week. Now, this was a new

experience for me. Everything was a first as a professional, with a different light shining on it. There was a lot to do during the week leading up to the fight on Saturday. Monday was a gym day, which is called a shakeout session, because at this point I was not going to get any fitter in a week; it was about keeping my body loose and getting a light sweat on. There was a lot of hype around the show, which meant more media interviews and photoshoots to do too. Tuesday was the same again, with additional press and photographs. Wednesday was the public workout, which was designed to give people a taste of what was to come. It was at the National Football Museum in Manchester, which is a famous venue for these preliminary events and lots of big names have held their workouts there. A large crowd had gathered to watch me, and I felt so honoured to be there: working out in front of about five hundred people was a big deal.

Thursday was a press conference with my opponent where we mainly talked about slaying each other; these can often get heated, although this one didn't. Friday was the weigh-in, which is always pretty nervewracking, no matter how many times I have done it since. My weight has to be bang on, so I keep checking it before leaving the house because if I am even a pound over it's not good. I have to get the right scales and can have four or five to check obsessively and

Turning TNT

figure out whereabouts my weight is. This carries its own particular stress, because then you have to weigh in, in front of a lot of people, to confirm that the fight can go ahead. For this fight, the weigh-in was quite special, at a massive convention centre in a huge room with almost a thousand people watching.

The day before, I'd popped to the Trafford Centre to find something to wear for the weigh-in. When I say something to wear, I basically mean a pair of boxer shorts, because you have to get on the scales with as little on as possible. It was almost Christmas, so I went festive. Looking back, I don't know what I was thinking, but at the time the shiny, sparkly tight red pants with *Merry Christmas* around the waistband seemed like the perfect thing to wear. I chose to come out to the theme tune from *Peaky Blinders* and was introduced by my professional name of Tommy 'TNT' Fury.

I walked on, laughing, waving to the crowd, flexing my muscles and taking it all in, and Ricky Hatton joined me on stage. I was in great shape, full of energy and confidence, so it was a good feeling, and I hit the right weight of 12st 11lbs. I was in bed by 9 p.m. and got a great night's sleep, ready for the day ahead. Even though I was nervous, it wasn't like my very first fight, I knew what I was doing and how it would feel. I felt prepared for anything.

83

On Saturday, the morning of the fight, I ate five eggs, scrambled, with a liberal squeeze of tomato sauce on top and a big bowl of porridge oats with honey and peanut butter, for slow releasing carbs throughout the day. Unlike before my debut amateur fight, I was able to eat, and I also told absolutely everyone that I was fighting, so all my friends knew! I met up with six of them and we hung out together in Costa Coffee. I ate little and often throughout the day. I was back home by about 2 p.m. to put my feet up, watch some telly and have a bit of a sleep. In many ways, it was just a chilled Saturday, as long as I didn't think ahead to what I was going to be doing in the evening. I then had my customary meal of a jacket potato with cheese and beans, which I now have before every fight. I could feel the nerves beginning to build, but I didn't show them, I just talked myself through it all and stayed calm because I was determined to enjoy the experience. This was my first big fight and I knew it was really special so I didn't want anything to spoil it.

My kit bag was packed, and I was in the front room with Dad, Mum and Roman, waiting for the moment to go. Mum was really nervous; she had never been to one of my fights before because she couldn't cope with seeing me in the ring, but I begged her to come because it was my first professional fight and in our home city. Getting her to agree was a massive accomplishment, but to date, this is the only fight she has ever come to because she can't bring herself to watch. She may listen on the radio, but often she will just keep busy until it is over, and she always tells me to call her straight after, which I do, because I know it is agonising for her to wait until she can hear my voice and know that I am fine.

'OK, it's time to get this show on the road,' Dad said when it got to 5 p.m. and that's when the nerves really kicked in. I took a deep breath, gave Mum a kiss goodbye, then Dad, Roman and I left. We had to get there early to get ready, and she was coming on later with my friends. When we turned up at the venue, I couldn't quite believe it. At 21,000 seats, the Manchester Arena then had the biggest indoor seating capacity in the UK and, as we walked past the ring, there were strobe lights flashing everywhere. I looked around in awe and tried to imagine it full of people watching me, before we went to the changing room, where I could start stretching and shadow boxing. I got my hands wrapped, my kit on and then the gloves so I could hit the pads, warm up and get a sweat on. By this point Ricky Hatton and my brother Shane had also joined us. I felt sharp and powerful on the pads; it felt good.

The fight was on TNT Box Office pay-per-view and also live on BT Sport, and there was a TV in the changing room so I could see the commentators talking about me as I was warming up. This was new and added a stressful dimension to proceedings. It was not something I thought I would be faced with for my first professional fight. Then there was a knock on the door and the two-minute call was given, like I was a rock star or an actor about to go on stage. I got my robe on, put my hood up, looked at myself in the mirror and said a little prayer before joining the rest of my team for a group prayer. My dad led it, as he still does to this day.

My religious beliefs come from my nana, although my whole family talk to God and Jesus in their own ways. I used to go to St Peter and Paul's Catholic Church round the corner from where I lived and was baptised and confirmed there, so my faith has always been a significant part of my life. I will often pick up my rosary beads and the Bible. I always say 'God bless' as a way of saying goodbye to people, even those who come up to me in the street. I pray before every fight and, after every fight, I thank Our Lord and Saviour Jesus Christ. I don't believe any of this would be possible without him looking over me. I thank him at the end of every successful thing I do. I think faith and belief can take you in the right direction and it has given me strong family values and a moral compass to navigate my way through life. I don't often speak about religion in the media or publicly, but I am always vocal in thanking the Lord, our Saviour Jesus Christ, so I get him out there when I can. My faith is a personal commitment. It's how I live, and it is one of the most important things in my life.

The fight crew came for me. There were cameras following my every move and a guy with a script was telling me to wait before the signal to start walking. My heart was racing so fast I thought it would burst out of my chest and they would capture the whole thing on film. I had imagined this moment so many times and here it was. From a fifteen-year-old amateur swinging through his first fight, to four years later as a professional at the Manchester Arena in front of thousands of people and screened live to however many more, how did I get here? What was going on?! This doesn't happen to someone like me, even though I had manifested it for a long time.

I stood there, the skinniest legs in the world sticking out of white, red, gold and black shorts, which were admittedly quite short, and my feet in red Nike boots. My gloves were black with gold detailing and my long robe combined all the colours with 'TNT' on the back of it. It was a strong look and I felt confident as I put my hood up and walked through the corridors to the ramp where I was instructed to stop before the MC introduced me. My team were with me behind the curtain and I was tapping my gloves together, trying to get into the right head space. I was at peak nervousness by this point and suddenly all the stress thoughts were rushing through my head, but I still believed that I could do it. I was carrying the family name into the ring and with that came the pride and commitment to keep our reputation intact. Tyson had put our name in the global boxing history books and taken it to heights it could never have reached without him. Please, God, let me not be the one to unravel his work. Please, God, let me not embarrass anyone. Please, God, let me take every second of this in. Please, God . . . The MC interrupted.

'And fighting out of Manchester, England, please welcome Tommy "TNT" Fury!'

The curtain was pulled back and I walked up the ramp to Womack & Womack's 'Teardrops', which may sound like an odd choice, but I love the oldies and didn't want to come out to rap or heavy metal. Besides, I chose that song for Mum because she always used to play it and loved it, so it felt like a little message to her in that moment. I knew she would be sitting in the crowd with her heart in her mouth and I wanted her to know I was thinking of her.

I looked around at thousands of people screaming and going crazy, and I could see my opponent in the ring already. I stood there for ten seconds and thought

Mum and Dad in their younger days.

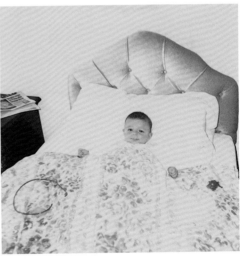

In my favourite place still to this day – bed!

Me as a baby with a cheeky smile.

My older brother Roman and me with our grandad.

Roman and me during our
primary school days.

Roman and me at Christmas –
butter wouldn't melt.

Mum, Roman, me and our friend Chris in my nana's garden enjoying a barbecue.

Me on my first P&O cruise!

Canaries Taster 25 April - 6 May, 2004

Aurora - The Dining Experience

A family photo on the cruise. Everyone enjoyed it so much that it became our yearly holiday.

Me as an altar boy with Father Joseph at St Luke's Catholic Church.

Kicking back in the hot tub. Not a care in the world. Those were the days.

The first time I met Molly.

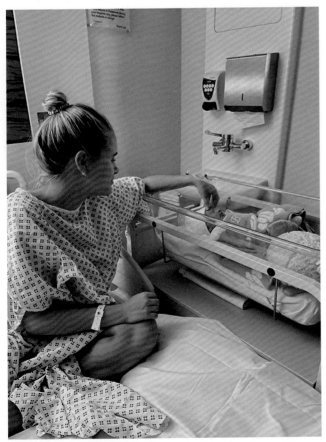

Hours after Molly had given birth to our beautiful angel.

Bambi and Molly with my grandad.

My dad and Bambi –
my, oh my, she was small.

Morning cuddles with my girl.
How I like to start every day.

When I won a teddy bear for
Bambi at Disneyland.

My soulmate and me at Bambi's first birthday.

Christmas time at the Fury household. Molly and me with matching PJs and little Bambi looking on.

back to all the times I got the bus, trying to make my way, feeling sorry for myself, the trials and tribulations, and the dream I'd always had of this moment. As I was thinking about those things, I grew into the event. The nerves disappeared. I was playing to the crowd, gesturing, I was shadow boxing: I felt great. Dad pulled me in to him before I got in the ring.

'Stay nice and relaxed, keep calm, I am here, you have got this, it's easy, show him what you are made of,' he said. And then I jumped through the ropes, and I was there in the spotlight, gladiator ready.

I did my traditional warm-up of jogging to one side of the ring, leaning back and bouncing on the rope and then to the other side to do the same before going to my corner. Robe off, limber up, lock eyes with my opponent and then glare! When the MC introduced me – 'fighting out of the blue corner from right here in Manchester, Tommy "TNT" Fury!' – the crowd went wild again because anyone fighting in their hometown gets a good reception. I heard all my mates, and I looked up to see them there in the stands with my mum, who had her head in her hands because she couldn't watch. I gave them a big wave. My opponent and I were called into the centre of the ring to listen to the referee, then we tapped gloves, walked back to our corners and said goodbye to our trainers as they jumped out of the ring. Now it was just me, my opponent and the referee. This is the moment when everything else gets blocked out and all my focus comes to this point in the ring. The crowd disappeared and I could hear a pin drop inside my head. Seconds out, round one, *ding ding* and go!

As soon as I got out there, I started enjoying it. I was feinting him, confusing him with my movements, kidding him into thinking I was swinging in with a punch. I could see in his eyes that he was really thrown by my behaviour and the use of a trick I had been taught in the Fury family training sessions. Dad always says that movement is everything, and this was key to my approach. I got my jab going relatively quickly, started pumping it out so it was landing nicely, with the odd right hand behind it, which gave me a chance to suss him out. What did he have in him and how could he get to me? It was tidy boxing and I felt like I was doing well. I didn't take any punches off him in the first round, and I managed to control the distance.

I had honed my professional style during a year of intense training, and I was loose and relaxed – quite different from how I boxed as an amateur. This was an opportunity to show the real me. I was enjoying myself because I knew it was my first professional fight, you only get one debut and I had to make the most of it. If I could do what I had done in training, in the face of all the pressure and under those big lights, then I would be a happy man, and I was. I went back to the corner after the first round and Ricky Hatton was ready with some wise words.

'You got the power on this guy. It is all there for the taking, so go out and put a bit more pressure on him.'

I nodded. I knew I wasn't going to lose: I just had a feeling, which had been with me from the moment I stepped inside the ring. I was supremely confident, exactly what I needed to be.

In the second round, I started throwing hooks to the body which I could tell were hurting him and he was reddening up, all around his sides, so I knew my punches were doing damage. This was what Ricky had asked for and I was giving it to him. When I went back to the corner he was pleased.

There was more of the same in the third round, with me piling on the pressure to try and take my opponent down and get a stoppage win. As I was sitting in the corner, waiting for the fourth round, I thought how much I would love a knockout in my debut, but also remembered the advice I had been given about not going out looking for it. I needed to box my best and not be distracted, and I had to remind myself of this.

The fourth and final round was about throwing everything at him, while keeping my composure, remaining smart and being aware of what could be coming back my way. We went the full four rounds. I won every single one, avoided getting hit, and I knew I had put in a great performance against an opponent of steel with much more experience than me. When my arm was raised and I was declared the winner, I felt incredible. It was different from the first fight when nobody was there because this time my dad was ringside and my mum, friends and people from my city were watching. It was a dream come true, and it validated the decision I'd made when I was drowning in the school system. In that moment, I thought I could do anything; I was invincible. To this day, aside from having my daughter and being a father and partner, it is the best feeling I could achieve in my entire life. Nothing else compares to the moment when your arm is raised at the end of the fight, when everything you have worked for has paid off. It is probably why so many boxers find it hard to call it a day: to say goodbye to that adrenalin rush is almost impossible to do – it becomes an addiction.

I sat down on the ring apron and was interviewed live, thanking my team and saying this is the start, I am here to be world champion. Everyone was congratulating me, and someone said I would never have knocked my opponent out, that even if I had fought him with a hammer in my hand, he still wouldn't have gone down. He was tough, but I won.

Back in the changing room, Dad was all smiles. I always go off his feedback and if he is happy with my performance, so am I. Whatever my dad doesn't know about boxing isn't worth knowing, and his is the only opinion that really matters to me when it comes to the sport. My mates piled in to see me, so I got dressed and we went straight out into Manchester, which turned into a rather eventful night. I was on an absolute high and I didn't want to let go of the evening; I wanted it to carry on for ever. Everyone was there for me, drinking, partying and celebrating because of something I had done. I don't usually seek to be the centre of attention; I am more comfortable congratulating others, but it's nice to get recognition for what you do, particularly when it means so much and you've had to bust your ass and risk injury to get there. It was very messy – we danced for hours and necked all the shots – and I finally stumbled home at 5 a.m. Amazingly, after a very rare night out, I didn't feel too rough in the morning!

I have really good friends around me, and I can count them on one hand. I trust them with my life, they have always been there for me, they understood my constant absences because of training and they have kept me grounded throughout everything. They care about me. When I had no money they would pay for me if we did go out, so it's good to be able to repay them now, like I did Chris after our Greek holiday. He is the same age as Roman, and they were in the same class together at school. Their friendship blossomed first and then, as I got older, we all hung out together.

Chris is a hard-working primary school teacher who teaches Year Six and recently took a job at the primary school we all went to, alongside some of the teachers who taught us. Which is where I met Kyle, when we were five, and here we are, still best mates twenty years later. He has two kids and is a personal trainer who often works with me as my strength and conditioning coach. He is brilliant at his job, and I would rather work with someone I know and trust – it also means I get to travel with my best mate, so it's a win-win for us both. And then there are my brothers; I am close to them all. Roman came into boxing later than me, jumped straight into the professional ranks a couple of years ago and since then he has had four fights and four wins. He is in every camp I am in, and we train together; it's great to have him with me too. Everyone is doing well, and we are fiercely protective and supportive of each other, no matter how different our lives are. Family comes first.

I didn't have a 'normal' teenage experience, but I haven't sacrificed my entire youth to boxing because I am still young. I can now afford to go out for a pint, and I know how to enjoy my time off. I try and meet my friends each week, whether for food, a game of pool or a swift half at the pub if I am not training, and we go away on city breaks. These friendships, and the time we spend together, are really important to me. No amount of success would make up for not having my mates by my side.

A small downside to my life now is that it's impossible to go for a big night on the town with friends without any hassle because I often get people shouting abuse, trying to catch me out, make a scene or film me drinking. I know this comes with the territory, but it doesn't make for a relaxing evening! So, I don't go out partying in public much, and if I do, I may hire somewhere for the night so it's private – otherwise it's not worth the stress. I'm in my mid-twenties and want to go out, but I have come to terms with life being different, and now I'm a father it's changed anyway. Had I known what was ahead of me, maybe I would have enjoyed myself a bit more without the glare of the spotlight or the phone cameras pointed in my direction. But hindsight is a wonderful thing – I don't dwell on any of it. It is what it is.

5

Blinded by Love (Island)

I walked onto the terrace, looked in the corner, saw Molly sat in the hot tub and thought, Oh my God, yes. I had never seen anyone who was more my type. I couldn't believe my eyes. It was as if the production team had waved a magic wand.

My life was about to change for ever in ways I had never envisaged, triggered randomly by a media day at Ricky Hatton's gym, where Ricky and I were filmed in the lead up to my professional debut. The idea was to film me hitting the pads while Ricky was interviewed about my progress. One of the questions was about me coming from a boxing family and Ricky came back with a hilarious response.

'He doesn't look like Hughie, he doesn't look like Tyson, he looks like he has just come off *Love Island*.' After the interview, we laughed about it and the name stuck; even the big, scary boxers at the gym called me Mr *Love Island*. I had never watched the programme, but I knew what Ricky meant and I didn't mind the nickname. I took it to mean that I looked after myself and was a fan of personal grooming, which was all true, rather than being a lothario, which I most definitely wasn't.

A few weeks later, after a gruelling training session in the gym and the clock ticking down to my debut, I was in the shower. The gym receptionist popped her head around the changing room door and shouted out that if I was in there could I make it quick. This had never happened to me before; I thought I was in trouble. I hurried out and she said she had just had ITV on the phone, and they wanted me to call them straight back. What on earth was this all about? I returned the call and spoke to someone in production who said they had seen the Ricky Hatton interview and taken a look at my Instagram account.

'We think you would be a perfect fit for the next series of *Love Island*,' the voice said persuasively. I was speechless. They wanted to know if I had watched it and I said I hadn't, so they told me to catch the high-lights and let them know what I thought. I put the phone down, immediately looked it up on YouTube and knew it wasn't for me. There just seemed to be loads of pretty lads trying to flirt with loads of pretty girls while being constantly filmed, and some of them were even trying to get their leg over on camera. Imagine what my mum and nana would say!

I called them back and said thanks, but no thanks. I had my first professional fight coming up in a few weeks and I needed to focus on my training, the event and then the next fight. I was a boxer, not a reality TV contestant.

'Let us know if you change your mind,' they said. Thanks, I thought, but I won't, and off I went to win my first fight in December 2018.

My second fight was at Morningside Arena in Leicester in March 2019. It was almost as big as the first one.

The opponent I was scheduled to fight pulled out on the Thursday of fight week, so at the last moment they found someone else for me to face. My new opponent, Callum Ide, had a good track record, so great in fact that Dad thought I was being stitched up. He was dead set against me fighting, saying I was only a novice, I had prepared for a different guy and that I was going to swerve this. We had been in the

Holiday Inn in Leicester since Monday, and I went to bed on Thursday night thinking I wouldn't be fighting on Saturday. It was such a depressing anti-climax after two months of nothing but a punishing training schedule, which now felt like a complete waste.

When I woke up on Friday morning, my mind was made up. OK, so yes, the guy I was supposed to fight had pulled out, but someone else was willing to step in, and if it made it a harder fight, then so be it, I was ready. Dad came into my hotel room, and I told him my decision, which was difficult because I have always followed his advice and I was about to go against it. He tried to talk me out of it, convinced there was some game-playing from the other side, but I dug my heels in.

'I know, but I want to fight.'

'OK, if you do, you do,' he said. And that was it. The fight was on. We alerted my brothers and friends who we had told not to bother coming, and now we said, get down here quick, the fight is back on! Tyson had been out of the country for my first professional fight, so he wasn't going to miss this one.

The build-up on the night was very similar to the first fight, and all my preparations were becoming traditions that I was too superstitious to let go of. I knocked him down once and he got back up and then I knocked him down in the same area again and he went down and stayed down. The fight only lasted forty seconds. I couldn't believe it. It was my first knockout, and everyone went mad, most of all me. I spat my gum shield out and threw it into the crowd, like anybody wanted it! I was so full of adrenalin, I was beating my chest and raising my glove. Tyson was jumping up and down and my friends were yelling in delight. That feeling was amazing, and it didn't go away for a while because a knockout is quite something, in a 'chest puffed out, feeling good about yourself' way. Which is terrible because the other person isn't feeling good about themselves, but that's the game. That's the world of boxing. I heard that my opponent was OK apart from a couple of broken ribs, which is why he hadn't been able to get back up. As soon as you know the other person is fine then the celebrations can begin in earnest.

We ran around Leicester like wolves in a forest, no shirts on, lining up pints of Guinness in what was becoming the standard procedure after every fight. There were a few unhappy bouncers that night, not that we did anything wrong; we aren't the sort to go looking for trouble, we were just a bit of a rowdy handful. Other than the incident over the ping pong game at school, I have never had a fight outside the ring. I needed a release after months of training, no booze, a big fight and a win. I couldn't just go back to the hotel and get into bed with the amount of adrenalin coursing through me; I needed to have some fun.

My third fight was scheduled for the summer of 2019, and I was training hard when it got cancelled. This was so frustrating, and I asked Ricky what I should do. He said to keep on training in case something came up. The rest of the year was stretching out ahead of me with no point to aim for and I felt like I needed a break, maybe a couple of weeks in the sun, but I didn't have any money for a holiday. The idea of *Love Island* suddenly popped back into my head. Perhaps it was fate that the fight was cancelled, and this might be an opportunity I shouldn't miss? After all, you only live once, and here was a chance to step out of my comfort zone. I thought about it for a couple of days and discussed it with Mum, who was nervous about the thought of me taking part. The more I considered it though, the more I realised I wanted to do it for me, and Mum understood and told me if that was the case then to go for it. I called ITV, told them what had happened and asked if I was too late to put myself forward. Luckily, they were still keen to have me.

Within a few days I was travelling first class by train to London, a place I had never been to on my own, in a carriage I wouldn't have been able to afford. All I had was some loose change in my pocket. I went to ITV and met the producers, directors and managers, and all of them were jolly and supportive, which was reassuring. Every single aspect of this was new to me and I couldn't get my head around it. What was I doing there? It felt strange, but not bad strange, just weird to step out of my very familiar world into unchartered territory. On the train home I felt at peace with my decision.

Before I left for *Love Island*, I had to keep it quiet, as any mention of it anywhere would undermine my position in the show. I knew that if it was leaked it would be over for me. I told my immediate family that I was going on, with the caveat that whatever they did, they must not tell anyone I was doing it because I would lose my place. Cut to me, in the gym one day, scrolling on my phone to see Tyson doing an ESPN interview which was going out globally.

'Big shout out to my brother, Tommy! He's going on a TV show called *Love Island*. He's a good-looking young kid and I think he's going to be a hit with the ladies on it. He clearly doesn't look like me because I look like an ogre!' he said at the end of the interview.

My heart sank. I thought, That's it, it's all over. I kissed the thought of a sunshine minibreak goodbye and mentally prepared to be ditched before I had even left the country. The next day ITV called me to say they had seen the interview and not to worry about it. Maybe it fell into the category of all publicity is good publicity, or perhaps it was too late to replace me, but whatever the situation, I wasn't going to question how I had got away with it – it was just a relief that I had. I was also relieved to get Tyson's support because when we had initially discussed the possibility, he wasn't sure it was a good idea and was worried it may have an adverse effect on my career and long-term goals.

'You're on a roll,' he said, 'keep with boxing.' What if he was right and this TV show was going to damage my reputation? But there was only one way to find out and it wasn't by sitting at home.

I had an inkling of what I was letting myself in for the night before I flew out to Majorca. The production team had put me up in the Lowry, one of the poshest hotels in Manchester, and Mum and Nana drove me there and dropped me off outside. They were both anxious about what I was getting into and weren't convinced about me doing it. That said, they didn't try and stop me. We sat in the car talking and it took them an hour to go because they didn't want to leave me. I understood their concerns, but it was too late to pull out and besides, I didn't want to. Just the thought of a free trip to Majorca was enough to keep me going, I didn't think too much about what I had to do once I was there. I went to the front desk to check in and was taken up to a suite. I was used to sleeping next to the boiler at home and suddenly there I was, in a fancy hotel, in an amazing room, ordering room service. I was in my element. This alone was worth saying yes to ITV!

The next morning, I met the chaperone who would be looking after me before the show, and we flew out to Majorca. Once I was there, I had to go into lockdown for a couple of weeks without any form of communication – my phone and even my watch were confiscated – and I wasn't allowed to mix with anyone. I was kept in a bubble. There were much harder ways to spend a fortnight – this in itself felt like a holiday after all the training and I took it all in my stride. It probably helped that I was totally clueless about what to expect because I hadn't watched the show and I thought I could wing it, so I didn't feel nervous. I was so convinced I would be out after a few days that I only packed four outfits and a couple of pairs of trainers, which ultimately meant the longer I stayed in the more clothes I had to borrow, and I was washing my boxers on a regular basis! I assumed I wouldn't be in for long. Before I left the UK, I had been for a drink with Kyle and we made plans to go out on my return, which we figured would be imminent.

When I walked into the villa, and onto camera, for the first time it was quite a moment. I had made an effort with a fresh haircut and my eyebrows had been done. I looked like an Italian mobster with my hair gelled, a little beard and a deep tan after two weeks spent soaking up the sun in lockdown. I thought I looked the bollocks! I arrived with the dancer Curtis Pritchard, who became a firm friend while I was in the house and we have kept in touch ever since. We both have well-known brothers too: his is A.J., one of the professional dancers on *Strictly Come Dancing*. The show had started earlier that day, so we came on in the evening as the 'bombshells', a little double surprise to keep everyone on their toes. A few of the contestants already knew I was joining the show after Tyson had blurted it out in his interview, and they told the others who I was. For a moment, it felt like I was a celebrity in there and all the girls were looking at me as if they were supposed to recognise me as someone famous in the outside world. I thought, If you only knew how much of a nobody I really am!

I knew I had made the right decision to come. The villa was stunning, the weather was incredible, and I was meeting some great people. I was the youngest there, but I didn't feel it considering how much I had done in my life already – apart from in the kitchen, where my cooking inexperience showed when I made breakfast. They were such a lovely bunch to hang out with, including a few boys who were into training and exercise like me. It was a reassuring start. I thought, I will be happy if I can spend a few days here, and if my luck stretches to several weeks then the job's a good 'un! I didn't want to leave, it felt like I was in the middle of a perfect daydream. I just wanted to be myself, have fun and clock up a new experience before I got back to my day job.

My villa mates had watched all the past series, so they understood the running order and the tricks of the show. All I knew was it was about finding someone you were compatible with, and I thought that would be a long shot for me, but for as long as I was in the villa, I was going to enjoy all of it. I didn't, for a single second, expect to meet a girl in there who I would have a connection with. I mean, who on earth goes on to *Love Island* to actually find love?! I thought the most that would happen would be a nice flirtation and some great friendships. Neither did I want to make a big personality splash. It wasn't in my nature to stir the pot and I avoided as much of the confrontation as possible. I wasn't there to be a larger-than-life character, that's not who I am, and because of being reticent in this and in love.

Four days after the start of the show, we were all sitting around the firepit when my *Love Island* phone bleeped.

'Got a text!' I shouted. It read:

Tommy, the public have decided you should go on a date with me. I am waiting for you in the hot tub on the hideaway terrace. Get your swimwear on and come and join me, lots of love, Molly-Mae x.

Everyone jumped around, yelling at the top of their voices. I was ecstatic. The public had voted for me to go on a date with the new girl, Molly-Mae. So far, there hadn't been a girl on the show who I had really clicked with, even though I'd been coupled up with Lucie who was lovely. I knew we wouldn't be more than friends so I was excited to meet the 'bombshell' before the others. I put on the tightest pair of black trunks I could find and some of the guys walked me to the door that led on to the terrace. Before I went through, I dropped down and did close to one hundred press-ups. I kid you not. Veins out, chest like breasts, I wanted to look muscular. I was filled with adrenalin, and everyone was laughing so I told them to leave me alone and let me get in the zone, like I was about to get in the ring. I walked onto the terrace, looked in the corner, saw Molly sat in the hot tub and thought, Oh my God, yes. I had never seen anyone who was more my type. I couldn't believe my eyes. It was as if the production team had waved a magic wand. She was nervous too, as it was her first appearance on the show and the rest of us had had four days to settle.

Molly invited me to join her in the hot tub, saying it was kinda cosy, and as I stepped in, I made a joke about falling into the water. She reached out her arm saying, 'Come to me' and we had an awkward kiss hello on the cheek before I scooted to the opposite corner of the tub. I did the worst flirting ever. She said my 'ocean' eyes were amazing and I said, 'Likewise, you are amazing'. It's one thing being filmed flirting, but another thing when your stomach is doing flips because it turns out you really like the person. I told her she was totally my type, and we discovered the first thing we had in common was that we were both twenty with May birthdays. And then that we lived in Manchester – Molly had moved there a few months before. I was astounded that she had been right there in front of my nose, and I didn't know it. Every time I was on my way to the gym on the bus, I would pass her apartment and I wondered how we had not bumped into each other on nights out. Possibly because I didn't go out very much, but still.

We hit it off instantly and the conversation flowed. Molly told me she was a social media influencer but had worked in a gym before that so there was yet more connection. I lost the little cool I had left and told her she was my ideal woman and listed her attributes just to underline the point. In what was probably a cringey screen moment, I gave her a flower and we toasted each other with a glass of fizz. There was something about that meeting that felt important, but I couldn't explain it. I said while I wasn't going to claim I had found my future wife (I know, totally crazy considering what has since happened), she was definitely my type and I asked her what her first impressions were of me, to which she said I was chatty before ... damn ... we were interrupted by another text. My turn was over, and she had to choose someone else to join her in the tub: #takeyourpick #oneoutonein. My heart sank, I was gutted, and I knew Molly was watching my reaction closely. She decided to go for Curtis, and I was magnanimous and said he was a lovely lad – the best lad in the house in fact – then I got out of the hot tub, taking my time towelling down so I could chat to her for longer. She knew I was smitten. I said on camera straight after that she went through my heart, did a 360 spin and then came back through my head. I was intrigued to get to know her more.

I returned to the garden of the villa and talked it all through with one of my fellow contestants, Liverpudlian Michael Griffiths, who is such a great guy and still a good friend of mine. I wasn't comfortable about Curtis sitting in the hot tub with Molly, but there was nothing I could do about it.

'She's the one,' I said confidently to Michael, 'she's amazing. I don't want anyone else.' This was after a twenty-minute conversation.

When Molly came into the house later that evening, she was sitting around the firepit with some of the girls, talking about who she liked. She had been worried that she usually picked bad boys and that I may fall into this category, but after spending time with me she didn't think this was the case, and the other girls were lovely and said that wasn't who I was. This is a fair assumption considering my day job, but it is not who I am at all. The next morning, I taught her how to spar using a pair of flip flops as pads, and we hung out together for part of the day. That evening was a recoupling and Molly had a choice to make. I had no idea who she would go for, and I felt the most nervous I had in the house. Thankfully she picked me, and after only twenty-four hours of knowing each other, we were sharing a bed. On the outside, if you meet someone you usually go on a fair few dates before you get into bed together, but we were thrust straight into an intimate environment and had it been anyone else I think this would have felt really strange. It was very unlike me. Plus, I like to spread out when I am in bed and need a lot of space – a bit of star-fishing – but it just felt right to be with Molly, cuddling until we fell asleep.

The days passed and we grew closer as we found out more about each other. I knew I was beginning to fall in love with Molly, but I wasn't sure how much she liked me. She was the type of girl I would have dreamed about – beautiful on the inside as well as the outside, funny and smart – it felt like I was going out with a supermodel. We had a lot of fun together, both as a couple and in a big group. I could easily forget I was being filmed for a telly show, and I didn't find the cameras intrusive, nor did I have a problem with wearing a microphone because I wouldn't make sly remarks and had nothing to hide. The production team didn't come into the villa very much, so we really were left to get on with it. Other than breakfast, food was prepared for us and set up as an outdoor buffet where we could help ourselves. This also signalled a camera and mic break for an hour while we ate, but we weren't allowed inside the villa so there was nowhere to disappear to. In the evening, dinner was the same as lunch, with an hour off before we then got dressed up for drinks and drama. We were limited to a couple of drinks each, although Molly didn't drink wine, so I used to secretly have her quota too.

Saturday was a day off from filming, which was always welcome. There was a second villa, and each week the boys or the girls would decamp there for the day, to keep us separate so nothing happened while the cameras were off. When we were split up, we would all get a huge McDonald's and lounge around talking about very little as we weren't allowed to discuss the girls or how we felt. Again, this was a relief because we did a lot of that throughout the week, so we needed a break from relationship chat and villa gossip. We were back together in the evening, but not allowed to share a bed as couples, so the boys shared beds and the girls did the same. The producers didn't want to run the risk of missing anything.

Much of the time, I genuinely thought I was on holiday. I didn't want to go back to Manchester yet; I just wanted to revel in villa life which had everything I needed, including a small gym with weights, a swimming pool and thirty-degree heat. All I was going home to was being punched in the face, so I was in no rush. I think it's the first time I properly relaxed after years of relentless training.

It wasn't all plain sailing with Molly, of course. I think she was the only one who I argued with in the villa! We had a massive row one night about our heads being turned by other people and I felt Molly had been keeping her options open. Molly was upset and said she found it hard to talk about her feelings, but hoped spending more time together would make me trust our relationship. Social media picked up on this and it was referred to in one of the games the islanders played. There were comments about whether Molly was really into me, saying she was only with me because I was popular, and she had her eyes on the money. I wasn't interested in what other people had to say. I am a pretty good judge of character and I was the one in the house with her, so I knew how she felt about me. We didn't fake it. We had integrity about ourselves and our relationship. Our fledgling love was being tested all the time and we survived everything the programme and our own insecurities threw at us. We had such a great connection and brought out the best in each other. Every morning, I would wake up next to Molly and it would make me smile. I am not sure what I had done to deserve her.

Two weeks into the show we had our first kiss, which was eventful because we were in a hallway and the camera wasn't on us. It just felt right to do it, so I kissed her and I didn't think about whether we were being filmed or not. I just went for it, much to the frustration of the production team, who wanted to capture the special moment and asked me to do it again. I thought, I am not doing it again just so you can film it, I will do it when it feels right – but I also understood why it was a moment they wanted to catch so I took an opportunity when we were chatting in the snug and leaned in. At that point everyone saw us and started clapping, and that was it. We were together.

On one of our dates, we went horse riding. I had never been on a horse before, and I couldn't even work out how to climb up on it at first. I was sweating and completely out of my comfort zone. This didn't feel very romantic, but Molly thought it was hysterical and told me to relax. All the horse had to do was move his head and I gasped: I was convinced I was going to be thrown off. Molly had ridden as a child, so she was totally at ease in the saddle and her horse trotted off while mine stubbornly refused to move.

'You have to tap him,' Molly said over her shoulder, so I reached out and patted the horse's neck. I didn't realise she meant for me to use my heels. 'Just relax. Why are you holding on to the reins like that?'

'I am holding on for dear life!' I was petrified. It felt like we were in a Country and Western music video so I made up a song in that style and sang it as we trotted along.

'I feel like we are going to ride off into the sunset together and live happily ever after,' Molly said as I gripped the reins tightly.

'That's the plan,' I replied. Neither of us had any idea what life was going to be like outside the villa for us as a couple, but we were keen to find out. We decided we weren't going to pursue anything with anyone else, no matter who walked in.

The producers threw a spanner in the works at this

point. In each series, about halfway through, they select either the girls or the boys to spend some time in Casa Amor, a different villa, where new contestants join them and endeavour to form new relationships. At the same time, bombshells are brought into the *Love Island* villa in what is billed as the ultimate test. If the original Love Islander falls for their Casa Amor seducer, then they can bring them back into the main villa with them, immediately breaking their existing coupling. Or they can choose to return to the villa alone and face a nail-biting moment to discover if their original partner has decided to couple up with someone else in their absence. It's a big old roller-coaster of emotions and Molly and I were about to experience it: she was off to Casa Amor.

I hated being separated from Molly; it felt like I was missing my right arm. We had gone from being together every day for a month, sleeping, eating, even brushing our teeth together, and then suddenly we were apart. It was just for a few days, but I knew then my feelings for her were way more powerful than I could control. I missed her so much. I thought she felt the same way and I needed to trust this, but I couldn't rest entirely easy, nervous that I had misread the situation or that her perfect man would turn out to be someone who wasn't me. How did I know that she wasn't going to have her head turned? This was the point of the twist in the show, and I had been told that many couples fell at this hurdle.

Out of respect to Molly, and the new girls who had come into the main villa, I slept on the day beds outside at night because I wanted to make my intentions clear. Molly was the only one for me and nobody was going to change that. I chose to stay loyal to Molly in the hope she would do the same to me.

'She wouldn't do anything to hurt me, would she?' I was looking for reassurance from every other man in the villa as my head went round in agonising circles.

'No, you'll be all right, mate. You and her are sound,' they all said, but they didn't really have a scooby what was going on in the other villa. None of us did. I think they were sick of having the same conversation with me and I was exhausted by putting myself through the torture of it, so after a couple of days I let it all go. Her behaviour was out of my control, and all I could do was act in the way that felt right to me. The new girls were really nice and we had good conversations, but I wasn't interested in anything more and they all understood that.

On the night of the original girls' return to the villa, I stood and waited to find out if Molly would walk back in on her own or with a new partner. Little did I know then that she had also refused to share a bed with another boy at Casa Amor and had slept outside with a couple of the other girls who were also being faithful to their boys back in the villa (which was not reciprocated). Waiting for her, as the suspense built, I prepared myself for the worst as couples fell apart around me, and hoped for the best.

Molly returned alone and broke down in tears when she saw me standing there. She was so overtaken by emotion she stopped in her tracks and crouched down for a few moments. She had thought I was with someone else because her cuddly toy elephant, Elly Belly, wasn't on the bed, but I was clutching it, and we were waiting for her. Elly Belly symbolised our relationship and we made jokes about it being our 'baby'. Caroline Flack, the presenter, was lovely to us both and most of the girls were in tears as we reunited.

Being apart for that time had made us realise how much we cared about each other. Molly revealed that she could be falling in love with me, and I said I had already fallen for her. We were both so happy: we had passed the *Love Island* test and we still adored each other. When I wasn't near Molly, I didn't feel like myself. The next step was to ask her to be my girl-friend, which I did the very next night. I pulled Curtis to one side and told him it felt like the right time, it was all or nothing. We came up with a plan which involved me writing a letter as if it was from Elly Belly, but we had no pen or paper, so we tipped the girls' make-up on the floor to find an eyeliner pencil! At that exact moment, Molly came up the stairs, and we hid as she walked in to find the contents of the make-up bag strewn over the floor. I tucked myself into the wardrobe and luckily she didn't spot me; she cleared up the mess and went out again. I asked Curtis to write the letter and he said he couldn't spell because he was dyslexic and I said I didn't even finish school. I could have written it, but I had a million butterflies in my stomach which was stopping me from thinking straight, so Curtis took over.

We chucked a few rose petals around on the terrace to set the scene. I felt as nervous as I had done before my first fight. I found Molly and told her Elly Belly had something to say as Curtis gathered the others and whispered to them that I was about to ask her to be my girlfriend, so they stood and formed a love heart on the grass below. The letter said:

Dear Mummy,
  Daddy left me here in his best interests. He wanted me to tell you, you are his everything and I am going to leave it with Daddy so . . .

Molly looked at me, surprised and unsure of what was coming. I took over.

'On a serious note, you know how much you mean

to me, and you know you are the only girl for me. I wondered if you wanted to be my girlfriend?' I was so relieved to have said it.

She was happy and said yes, throwing her arms around me, and everyone cheered from their love heart on the grass.

One of the other best moments of the series was when my mum and Roman came on for the 'Meet the Parents' segment. As I have said, Mum hadn't been on a plane since she was a teenager, so I couldn't believe she had overcome her fears and was in the villa with me. It was so special to be able to hug her and hear her say she was proud of me, and to meet Molly's mum and sister too. Her mum congratulated mine on how well she had brought me up and Mum cuddled me and called me a 'Mummy's Boy', which I was fine with because I am! I really appreciated Mum being there.

On the outside, Tyson was also rooting for me.

'I thought, He's a good-looking lad,' he confessed in an interview at the time, 'he might get carried away being a TV reality star rather than a fighting man – and it's the last thing he needs to do when he's trying to become a professional fighter.' He admitted he had tried to discourage me from going on the series, but he then said I was 'smashing it'. I didn't see this interview until I had left the villa, but I really appreciated the support from him and the rest of my family, even if I didn't know about it at the time.

On our last date on the show, I walked into an incredible private dining room with Molly on my arm; she looked movie-star fabulous in a floor-length yellow dress. We were both emotional that we had reached the end and we had done it together. I hadn't expected this to happen. I really didn't think I would come out of the show with a girlfriend; I'd assumed nobody would be interested because I didn't think I was a great catch. I didn't party much, I didn't go out drinking, I trained most of the time and my job was to hit people, so I wasn't sure how Molly would feel once we left the villa. We talked about what was next, her watching me box, me seeing her in her element and the possibility of living together. It was a fairy-tale evening, Molly called me her Prince Charming and I whirled her around the dance floor. If I could have bottled that night, I would have done.

A couple of days before the final came was the moment when each of the remaining couples were asked to declare their love. It was incredibly romantic with the boys in super-smart tuxedos while the girls were stunning in amazing dresses. I stood in front of Molly with my speech written down on cards and I started to read from them before chucking them on the floor and saying . . .

'This isn't me. I want my heart to speak to you, not my mouth. From the first moment I walked up into the Hideaway, I instantly knew I had seen the most beautiful girl on this entire planet. It was like somebody had gone into my mind, reached in and grabbed my perfect girl and put her in that little corner of the hot tub. You're absolutely everything I've ever wanted in a girl. Every day I wake up and all I want to do is put a smile on your face. I thank you for making this the best summer of my life. You're honestly my everything. You're my entire world. And I'll love you until the day I die.'

And Molly said . . .

'Tommy. For someone whose career depends on fighting other people, you're the gentlest person I've ever met. You're my bestest friend and the most incredible dad to our Elly Belly. I genuinely believe that I am the luckiest girl in the world, and I am being loved in a way I have never been loved before. Thank you for showing me kindness and nothing but pure love every day, and thank you for making me realise that fairy tales really do exist. I can genuinely say I have never felt feelings like this in my whole life. I love you so much and I can't wait for the adventures that we haven't even dreamed of yet.'

Getting to the final was incredible, and doing it with Molly was the best feeling in the world. I knew the public must have been voting to keep us in, but I didn't know how big the show was or what people really thought of us. On the day of the final, we all got taken to a hotel before the evening show. The place was supposed to be empty and there was nobody in the hotel lobby when we walked in. Molly and I were waiting for the lift with the other finalists when the doors opened and a guy came out and stopped, staring at me.

'It's Tommy Fury!' he said, pointing at me. I was confused. How did I know him? Then I realised I didn't, but he knew me because he had been watching me on TV for the last couple of months. It was a taste of what was to come – although I didn't know that then.

We returned to the villa for the final show in front of a live audience of a couple of hundred people who were shouting out my name. There were three couples left with us – Amber and Greg, Ovie and India, Maura and Curtis – and then we got down to the last two couples, standing opposite Amber and Greg, as Caroline built tension before announcing the winners. It was hard to believe we were finally at the end of the experience. It was amazing and beautiful to go through the show with the girl I loved. Caroline declared Amber and Greg the winners and we were genuinely happy for them. Coming second was better than I had ever hoped for, and while we may not have walked away with the prize money, we had each other and the memories of a perfect summer. In that moment, I couldn't have felt luckier. We were living proof that *Love Island* really could work. We all toasted each other with champagne and hugged Caroline. Having Caroline there felt like a big sister keeping an eye on us all and I was so shocked and saddened to hear of her death less than a year later. She was a clever, funny, brilliant person to be around, with the biggest smile, and we were lucky to have got to know her a little and to have spent time with her. Caroline will forever be entwined in our incredible *Love Island* experience.

After the show, I was given my phone back. The production person who handed it over told me to switch it to aeroplane mode as soon I turned it on because the number of messages coming through would break it. I laughed.

'You're all right, mate, it will just be my mum and my nana who will call me.' He gave me a look that said, You have no idea. I didn't take any notice because I couldn't have imagined what was about to happen, and I turned my phone on. Within seconds it went crazy, like it had a life of its own, constantly buzzing. I had around seven hundred text messages, maybe eight hundred WhatsApps and countless emails and phone calls: there was no way I could respond to them all. It was impossible to keep up with all the comments, supportive messages and even famous people talking about me. How did they know who I was?! In the moment I didn't know what to think about it; I was completely stunned. For a reality TV show to have that sort of impact was beyond my comprehension. When I went on the show, I had about twenty thousand Instagram followers from my boxing career, and when I came out, I had more than 2.1 million. How do you get your head around that?

The night of the final, once everything was over, we all stayed in separate villas before heading to the airport the following morning. Molly and I were on our own for the first time and we couldn't begin to process the last twenty-four hours, let alone the previous ten weeks. Little did we know then, it was the calm before the storm. We were in bed, I turned on the TV, the news came on and a big headline read 'Fury Cousin in Stab Hell'. What the actual? Molly asked if it was anything to do with my family and I said I hoped not, but then my face appeared on the screen which was totally surreal. I got on the phone to my dad, and he told me my cousin Peter, one of Uncle Peter's sons, had been stabbed more than twenty-five times in Alderley Edge. He was lucky to be alive and made a full recovery, but it was awful for him, and our family and I was so glad to be heading home the next day.

We flew back to the UK and when we got off the plane at Stansted, it was like we were the Beatles. The airport was filled with thousands of people, media and news crews. People were trying to reach us, climbing over railings, and grabbing at us as well as chanting our names and asking for autographs. None of us had any idea this would be the reaction; it was a massive deal for us all. Like going from zero to two hundred miles an hour in super quick time. Before *Love Island* I was a boxer, with an overdraft, living at home with my family and I thought the show would be a free holiday, a laugh and a way to fill some time that had become available. Suddenly I had some money, offers of work, an unbelievable social media following and a girlfriend. Overnight, I had turned into a sort of celebrity, and I wasn't sure how I felt about it.

6

Fighting Talk

*I appreciated what the reality TV world
had given me, and there were so many
benefits to my growing profile, but that
wasn't what motivated me to get out of bed
in the morning. It was my boxing career
that did that. I knew if I could find a way of
combining both jobs then there would be no
stopping me.*

There was my life before *Love Island*, and then there
was the life that came after it. I hadn't changed but
so much around me had, and some of it not for the
better. When we arrived in Stansted, I was supposed
to be going back with Molly, to her mum's house,

which was quite close by, but instead I was met by my dad, Roman and a few friends. As well as the news about my cousin, Dad told me my grandad was in hospital after a stroke. At the happiest point of my life, the bad things were still happening: my joy didn't protect anyone else. It was gutting to hear about Grandad and how poorly he was, and we drove straight to see him in the hospital in Manchester, the same place he had dedicated his life to for many years.

I spent an hour or so with him and it was a shock to see how badly his speech and mobility had been affected. For this to happen to someone as outgoing and sociable as him felt cruel and unfair. He was the life and soul of the party who loved a drink, a laugh and an evening playing snooker, and that is how we knew him. Yet, here he was, stuck in a hospital bed and barely able to communicate. It was heartbreaking. I had just had this strange, wonderful experience and one of the people I most wanted to share it with and make proud was him. He has always been like a father to me and was one of my idols, there for me through everything.

Grandad came home after a few weeks and, to this day, he is only marginally better, which still takes me by surprise because the man he is now is not the man he is in my mind. It is much harder for him to communicate, and we can't share big conversations together like we used to as he gets tired very quickly. This is something we have all had to come to terms with and we are just grateful that we still have him with us, which is a blessing.

From the hospital, I went home to see the rest of my family – my mum, nana and auntie – and we all chilled out together. We didn't go out that night to celebrate my return because everything was weird. Not only was I coming to terms with my grandad's illness, I was also recognised in the hospital and on the street, so I didn't want to risk going to a pub. Everyone was happy I was back, and I know Mum had struggled with me being away for so long, especially because we had no contact. I had never been apart from my family for more than a week, and that was only once to go to Greece. At least they had been able to see me on ITV2 every night at 9 p.m., but I couldn't see them and it was tough not knowing how anyone was.

The first few days back were a surreal mix of great and awful. It should have been an exciting time, and in some ways it was, but I was missing Molly, who was still at her mum's, and I was popping to the hospital every day to see Grandad. After one visit, Roman and I went to the Trafford Centre. We were both feeling really low and sat drinking in a bar for hours, not enjoying ourselves, just trying to get our heads around the new reality and numbing the sadness.

After the first couple of weeks, with the novelty of some money in my pocket, I took my mum out for lunch. We decided to go to YO! Sushi in the Arndale Centre. It was midweek so I was counting on it being fairly quiet because I had experienced a lot of attention since I had been out of the villa, but this was the first time Mum and I had been out together. The low-key lunch I'd hoped for was not to be. I was stopped constantly by people asking for photos and wanting to chat, so what should have been a five-minute stroll took an hour. Mum was laughing, she couldn't believe it!

'What the hell is going on, Tommy?' She was gobsmacked. 'Does this mean you have made it?!'

'Mum, I don't know, I have no idea what is happening. It's mad! It's all new to me as well.' I wasn't sure I would ever get used to strangers coming up to me like they knew me.

There was more interruption in the restaurant, but I didn't care because apart from everyone being nice, what made me really happy was being able to treat Mum to a meal out. I had never had any money before so it had usually been her looking after me, but now I could spoil her. It was my turn to do something lovely for her. I don't think either of us thought it would last, so it felt good to make the most of it. While my family were proud of my time in *Love Island*, they all expected me to be back in the gym within the month.

After a week I met up with Molly for some post-*Love Island* filming and then she came to the gym I trained in for another filming segment. It was so good to spend time with her. She moved back to her flat in Manchester, and we saw each other every day. We were both really busy, but we grabbed time where we could and would go for something to eat or to the cinema, which gave us a bit of normality and a chance to date in a way we hadn't been able to do at the beginning. A month or so later, we moved in together into our first apartment in central Manchester, a couple of minutes from Molly's old place. I had gone from living at home with my parents, sleeping next to the boiler, to a four-bedroom duplex with the girl of my dreams. It happened pretty fast, but we both knew it was right. *Love Island* sped up our relationship: being together twenty-four/seven made a week in there more like a month on the outside. We knew everything about each other, which was funny because a couple of months previously we had been complete strangers.

It was a blessing that we didn't win *Love Island*. I think the winners face a lot of pressure to be the perfect couple and stay together. There was no expectation on us so we could build our relationship at the pace and in the way we wanted. When the show finished, we were free to go, but then the real heft as a couple began, because on the outside you can do whatever you like without cameras following your every moment. A lot of people split up, and only a few couples have stayed together beyond the first few months.

Before going on the show, I had been introduced to a manager who ran the contestants' social media, lined up deals and organised work for when they came out; I signed up because it was just part of the process. When we were in the villa, everyone was talking about what would happen to them afterwards as a result of the show and I was thinking, after?! I am going back to a sweaty gym, that's what I'm doing. I had no idea that brands watched the programme to see how the contestants conducted themselves and would decide whether they were appropriate to work with, as good representatives of their name and products. I didn't understand any of it and I hadn't a clue that you could earn money by posting about brands on Instagram. Prior to the show, my experience of sponsorship was when two local businesses put logo badges on my shorts and paid me a couple of hundred quid. That felt like the closest I would get to the big time!

I wasn't expecting the offers that came flooding in, nor the big money that was attached to them. I was being approached to model for clothing brands and to travel to far-flung places. It was like being in a movie, except it was real life and it was *my* life. There were public appearances (PAs) at nightclubs around the country where I would spend a couple of hours signing autographs and having photos taken before partying with the mates who'd come with me. They couldn't get their heads around how this had happened to me in such a short space of time. I was just Tommy to them, and thank God I was – and I still am. You survive these out-of-body experiences because those close to you keep you firmly rooted in reality. Even now, I never really get used to it, and back then I was expecting to pinch myself and wake up. It had been a hard slog for me to make it as a boxer and just as I was getting somewhere, this other part of my career was taking off. What did I even call myself? A sports influencer? A celebrity? I had no idea.

I had more than a hundred personal appearances booked across the country, a six-month modelling contract with the clothing brand boohooMAN, and big brands vying to work with me. I was dashing around, turning up at nightclubs at midnight to pose for selfies for a few hours and not getting into bed until around 6 a.m. I'd sleep until lunchtime and then be up working on all the other stuff that had come in, like Instagram brand deals, before heading to the next club. There was very little time to get to the gym. To begin with it was amazing. This was the sort of life that happened to other people, not to me, and I wanted to embrace everything about it, but I knew this wasn't the career I was meant for and nor was it a way for me to find true happiness.

While I couldn't believe I was being paid to turn up at nightclubs with my mates, be made a fuss of and have drinks bought for me, in truth the novelty wore off pretty quickly. After a while I just wanted to be at home. I had been on the road for a couple of months, and I wasn't happy. It feels ungrateful to say it, but it was exhausting: my body clock was skewed because I was up at night and sleeping in the day, I was surrounded by strangers, and everyone wanted something from me. I kept telling myself how lucky I was, and I also knew I couldn't give any more. I spent much of my time sitting in the back of a car, being driven down motorways to wherever the next venue was.

I was committed to attending the personal appearances from the summer to the end of the year, some as far away as Scotland and Ireland, and many down south. I had done about sixty, with forty to go, when I had a revelation. One October afternoon, I was walking around a random town, literally kicking a stone along the ground and waiting for the nightclub event later that evening, and I thought, What on earth am I doing? I am a serious boxer who had big aspirations only a few months ago, and now I'm drinking in clubs every night and signing pictures of myself. I had a conversation in my head about how long I could keep it up for and why I was really doing it. I could feel myself going down a road which really didn't suit me, and I thought, Nah, I can't do this anymore. I turned to the manager I had at the time, and I said, 'Listen, mate, you have to cancel the rest of these gigs, I am not interested, I am going back to the gym.' That night was my last event.

I may have stepped back from the personal appearances, but the phone continued to ring and I was still working with brands and really enjoying the experience. The first collaboration was a knockout. I was a massive mayonnaise addict and I loved Hellmann's, I had it on everything – burgers, steaks, eggs – you name it, I smothered it in mayo. A few weeks after I had come out of the villa, Hellmann's called and asked me to be in an advert with the promise of a lifetime supply of mayonnaise! It didn't get better than that. I had massive tubs of it stacked up in my parents' outhouse, and they gave me my own bottle which had 'Tommy's Mayo' printed on it.

I started my contract with boohooMAN around the same time. It was my debut modelling job and the first photoshoot was at their Manchester HQ, followed by more in London, Ibiza and Paris. I was clueless about posing in front of the camera and I had to get to grips with it fast, but I did and I had a great time doing it. There were other approaches, and I was careful to choose brands I liked, who were reputable and relatable to who I was. It was tempting to do everything and capitalise as much as possible, but I had my real career to protect and I decided to be strict about what I committed to, prioritising partnerships that were appropriate, on brand or fun to take part in.

One thing I did say yes to was an idea from ITV2 who really liked the friendship between me and Curtis Pritchard on *Love Island* and how he tried to teach me to dance while I would teach him how to box. He was definitely better at my job than I was at his! ITV2 approached us about a series centred around the two of us, *The Boxer and the Ballroom Dancer*, where we would step into each other's shoes and spend weeks training before taking part in a competition. Curtis was to fight in the ring, and I would enter a dance contest. At first, I wasn't sure I could do it and it felt like another step in the wrong direction for my boxing career, but then I thought we could have a bit of a laugh with it and Curtis agreed.

I was learning Latin and ballroom dancing with a professional dancer, Chloe Hewitt, at Curtis's parents' dance school on the Cheshire border, and Curtis went to Ricky Hatton's gym to train with a couple of my mates. We had six weeks training in each other's respective jobs, occasionally popping over to check in on how the other one was doing and give pointers. Curtis was doing much better than I was, although I came on really well, particularly in the tango, apart from nearly breaking my ankle several times and having to wear shiny dance shoes which made my feet look tiny. I had gone from a ghetto way of thinking to a ballroom philosophy, yet there were more similarities than you may think as both jobs require you to be super fit. In the past, boxers, perhaps most famously the Ukrainian Vasyl Lomachenko, have taken dance classes to prepare for fights because it helps with balance and footwork.

The fight was a week before my dance competition, so I went along to support Curtis who did brilliantly and won. Then it was my turn, and I really enjoyed the experience even though I didn't win. It was completely different from what I was used to; Chloe was great to work with and I was pleased I had taken it on, but I was definitely going to stick to what I did best. I am hopeful that some of what I learned won't desert me in the future, particularly for Molly and my first dance at our wedding, although that may not be the best time to pull out the tango.

The glitz, glamour and freebies of a celebrity influencer lifestyle were lovely, don't get me wrong, but I always had half a mind on boxing, that was my world, that was who I was, and I had to be able to go back to it with my head held high. I appreciated what the reality TV world had given me, and there were so many benefits to my growing profile, but that wasn't what motivated me to get out of bed in the morning. It was my boxing career that did that. I knew if I could find a way of combining both jobs then there would be no stopping me.

I was a professional athlete and that gave me the opportunity to earn good money and maintain a lifestyle doing something I was passionate about. Through Tyson, I had seen what boxing can do if you commit wholeheartedly to it. And thanks to *Love Island*, I now had the profile of a world champion, even though I wasn't, so that was what I wanted to work towards. To achieve the sort of career platform and recognition I now had would have taken around thirty to forty fights for most boxers, and even then, you are lucky if you get there. I had surpassed this in a few months without needing to take any blows to the face. Furthermore, I was earning proper money. I had been paid a few thousand for my first professional fight and similar for my second, but once I had covered my costs – gym fees, my support team, travel and food over ten weeks of training – it didn't leave me with anything. I think the most I ever seemed to have in my pocket was a tenner, and some of that was for the bus. For the first time in my life, I had a healthy bank balance. Did I need to be a boxer anymore? My head said maybe not, but my heart said yes, boxing is what you do and who you are. I didn't choose boxing for money or fame, I wanted to be a champion. My recent fights have been at championship level, with more pay-per-views than globally renowned bouts, so I have kind of done it but not done it. The only thing I don't have is a belt.

The morning after my final nightclub appearance, I went back to Ricky Hatton's gym. I walked in and everyone looked over and said, 'Oh, look who's back!' There was a lot of piss-taking, quoting me and picking up on stuff I had done on the show, and this went on for a good few weeks. I expected nothing less – it was all done in a playful and affectionate way. It felt so great to be back, and nobody's attitude towards me had changed; they weren't interested in where I had been or what suits I had been modelling. I just picked up where I had left off. And the brilliant thing about being in a boxing gym is that we may mess around, but we can't get away from the work: once you are in the ring and the bell goes, nobody cares who you are, it's the fight that matters.

After the first session back, I sat on the edge of the ring and thought, How the hell am I going to get back to where I was, fitness wise? Two rounds on the bag and I was blowing, whereas before I could do twenty rounds. This was what happened after four months of eating rubbish, drinking and late nights. It takes it out of you, even when you are young. It didn't matter that I was at peak fitness before *Love Island*, because without putting the work in it drops quickly and severely.

I got myself back into the routine. I would creep out of the apartment by 6 a.m. every morning, careful not to wake Molly, and go running. I could have had a lie-in and a lazy breakfast before starting the day, but that wasn't going to get my fitness back up. Instead, like the fourteen-year-old me, I imagined I had nothing, went out in the dark and pounded the streets of Manchester. Once I had got the run out of the way, I was free to work for the rest of the day and then I would train every evening. After a month or so, I was getting back to my old self.

My dad asked me how I was feeling, now I was training regularly, and when I wanted to fight. I thought about it. I had already had an amazing year so why not squeeze one in, in December, to end the year as I had started it?

'Let's go out with a bang!' I said.

'That's all well and good,' Dad replied, 'but you can't go around doing all these photoshoots and brand commitments and train for a fight at the same time.' I knew that. It was time to put boxing first again.

I went from living the high life to a serious regime. I started the training camp in November with Dad. I had been getting a bit of hassle at Ricky's gym because people had worked out I was there and were coming down to hang around, interrupt sessions and ask for photos. It was a distraction I couldn't afford, and it was annoying for other gym members. I left Ricky's on good terms, and he is still a great friend of the family, so there are no issues. I just needed a bit of privacy, and my dad knew exactly where I could find it. He had a mate, Arthur Little, a mechanic with a garage in Sharston, and above it he had built a gym called the Manchester Fight Club. It was funny because it wasn't really a gym that other people used, and nobody really knew it was there. It had all the kit – bags, mirror, weights and ring – and it was just me, my dad and Arthur. It was a fantastic secret gym. Nobody knew where I was training or would have expected me to be working out above a mechanic's. Nor did they think I would get back in the ring again, assuming my fighting days were over.

I trained harder than I probably ever have over those few weeks. I was a machine, ten times the man I was, even before *Love Island*. Now I had the confidence which came from the success of recent months. I also had some money so I could pay for the support I needed, like sports massages, saunas and cryotherapy.

I could afford to eat better, bought good quality meat, and I was getting proper rest too because everything was scheduled. I used the money I had earned from the work that came following *Love Island* to reinvest in the career I had wanted since I was a little boy, and that felt like another complete circle in my life.

I went to see Frank Warren again and this time Dad came with me. We sat around his table and worked out a date and a deal, settling on 21 December 2019, ten months after my second fight and almost a year to the day after my debut. I had started the year doing what I loved, and I'd make sure I ended it doing what I loved, with my ITV excitement joyfully filling the middle part. This time around was different with Frank. Things had changed for me, and we all recognised that. At our first meeting I had been like a stray dog waiting at the table for scraps and now it was us dictating what was going on and so we worked out a deal we were very happy with. I am not sure Frank was as happy with the sudden jump in negotiations, but he knew the attention I could bring and the number of tickets that would be sold, so it benefited him too. We announced it and everyone went mad. Nobody could believe I was getting back in the ring before the year was out.

My fee for boxing changed after *Love Island* because of my profile and I couldn't get my head around it. I went from a small fee to earning what world champions make and I was only fighting six rounds. It was a massive leap into big money. I still had no real idea about the hype around the show and it surprised me on a daily basis. When I did the public workout for my first fight after *Love Island* there were thousands of people – it was like a fight attendance. I appreciated them turning out to support me, but all I was doing was hitting some pads.

I was determined that I had to put in the best performance I could for this fight, as the stakes were higher than they had ever been. Winning would be the icing on the cake of an amazing year and I knew all eyes were on me, so I trained with that vision in mind. After a six-week training camp, I was as fit as fire.

The venue for the event was the Copper Box Arena in London and it was my first fight in the capital city. While the first and second ring walks had been a big deal, so much had changed since then, and I was now hot property. This time I felt like a world champion already. The place was full and there were no empty seats. I came out in a flashy white and gold kit with fur around the hood, dancing on the way to the ring to Michael Jackson's 'P.Y.T.', and everyone was reaching out to touch my glove. I had been on a run three weeks before and still didn't have a ring-walk song. I put on my playlist and when this song came on, I started sprinting. It turbo charged me and I thought, This is it. The song must have sounded the right note for the fight because it only lasted sixty-two seconds.

I was up against a fit guy from Poland, Przemyslaw Binienda, who had thirty fights to his name, so I was sure it would be hard going, but I just wiped him out. I didn't take one punch and didn't have a scratch on me. I came out and felt sharp; I could feel the win in me. He went to throw a hook and I leaned and came back on top with the right hand, and he crashed down to the canvas. He got back up and the referee signalled to continue so I went straight over to him and put a flurry of punches together before the referee stepped in, waving everything off, and I jumped up on the top rope. Again, like an idiot, I spat my gum shield into the crowd. I don't know why I thought anyone would want it; I'm not sure what goes through my head in that moment! The crowd were totally behind me – it was unbelievable. Everyone was cheering, and I was on cloud nine, it couldn't have gone any better. I was not expecting a knockout. As my first fight after *Love Island*, it was important for me to get in the ring as a boxer, so winning after a punch-perfect performance meant everything to me.

It was also the first fight Molly came to. She had never been to a boxing fight in her life, so she didn't have a clue what was going on. It was nerve-wracking for her, but it went so quickly she didn't have time to worry about me and she was ecstatic. She sat with Roman, my dad and my best mates and it made me think, I am not going down in front of the missus, no way! I could have fought the devil himself and beaten him. I wanted to impress her. The rest of my family were watching on TV and Tyson called me afterwards. We all went out and I remember somebody was wearing a T-shirt with my dad's face on; it was so random and also hilarious, and we couldn't work why they would have that, but I wanted one.

We headed to the Westfield in Stratford, to the bars and restaurants underneath the shopping centre, and we found somewhere to play ping pong, dance and drink before it closed at 1 a.m. Back at the hotel, the bar was open all night and I don't think we headed to our rooms until 6 a.m. I have got a picture from that evening, of a table full of empty beer and wine bottles, and it looks like a booze crime scene. It was only me, Dad, Roman and a few friends because Molly doesn't really drink. So much had happened that year we thought, why not? God has been great, let's celebrate together – and that's what we did. It was a brilliant night, but not so good when I woke up a few hours later and my head was pounding.

It had been quite a year. While so much had changed, I was still the same kid, and yes, there was a lot more attention on me, but it was nothing I couldn't handle, particularly as it meant I was able to do things I never thought I could do. At Christmas, I bought nice things for my mum and nana which was the best feeling. I was able to make other people happy. I have lived in Manchester my whole life and there are a lot of homeless people and charities that need support. When I was younger, I would pass people on the streets on my way to the gym and not be able to give them anything because I had nothing myself. Now I could, and that felt good after all those years of walking past with empty pockets. I could take my friends out to repay all the favours they had done for me over the years and afford a nice holiday with Molly too.

It was my first Christmas with Molly. She went off to her family on the twenty-third and I went home to see mine and then, on Christmas Day, after presents and a big lunch, I got a car from Manchester to Molly's for the evening. The following day we flew to the Maldives to see in the new year together and it couldn't have been a better way to end a mostly brilliant year. Thank goodness we did, as we had no idea how different the next year was going to be.

In March 2020, everything stopped. One minute, life was speeding along full of work, training and plans for future fights and then there was Covid. News of an impending lockdown made us think about where we wanted to be. In one way, being stuck in our city apartment would feel a bit like being back on *Love Island*, but as nobody was sure how long it would go on for, we were worried we might go stir crazy. We couldn't go to my parents' because there was no spare room, so Molly suggested going to her mum's, where we could hang out with her family and be close to the countryside. We stayed there for six weeks or so, until restrictions were relaxed. It was really sociable; we played games, watched films, walked every day and went to the corner shop. A simple existence and a very happy one. We knew it wasn't like this for lots of people, so we were grateful.

While my boxing career was on hold, the Instagram work continued, in fact it grew because everyone was spending a lot of time on social media. It became a bit of a lifeline for many and offered a way for us to connect with people while we were all trapped between our own four walls. I was really grateful to have this distraction and stream of income. Molly and I both turned twenty-one in May, and it was incredibly special to celebrate our big birthdays together, even though we couldn't go anywhere.

During this time, we knew we were the lucky ones. We watched the news and heard story after story of how hard it was for people in the pandemic: losing loved ones, mental health struggles, businesses closing, and children stuck in abusive environments without the sanctuary of school. Coming from a family of doctors and nurses, I knew the toll it was taking on the NHS too. That was the world we were living in. So, I know it sounds selfish to say I missed getting in the ring, but I did. After the novelty of the break wore off, I think many of us found it hard with no routine and no idea when our work and normal lives would begin again.

By the summer, things were a little easier, although it felt like restrictions were regularly changing (social distancing to bubbles to groups of six), wearing a mask was expected and we were all wary about what would happen in the winter, but didn't want to think about it too hard. Future lockdowns were discussed so we grabbed the opportunity to travel while we could. Sport was allowed again too, but without spectators. Dad and I worked out a deal with Frank Warren for a four-round light heavyweight contest against Genadij Krajevskij at the BT Sport Studio on 13 November. It was a fight behind closed doors – which meant no fans – but I was so happy to have a focus to my training and a reason to be getting back in the gym.

The latest Covid rule was that professional athletes were allowed to train, but commercial gyms were still closed. I could use Arthur's gym without fear of seeing anyone, which made social distancing very easy. It was perfect. I picked up the key from Arthur and got on with doing what I loved. On the Monday of fight week, we were in a fighter-only hotel, in a quarantine bubble with our small teams. We tested for Covid three times before the big day and were not allowed to interact with anyone externally. At the press conference, I spoke about why I was choosing to fight again.

'Everyone thinks I am playing and getting these fights in for a bit more fame, but that's not the case. I have been smashed to pieces in the gym and I know what it feels like to ship some hard punishment. I come from a fighting family, it oozes out of me, and I have the ability to go all the way.' It was so good to be back.

On the night, I was getting my hands wrapped and I could hear the music playing as usual, but the place was empty and silent; it was the strangest experience. After my third fight, in front of a packed house of thousands of screaming people, my fourth fight felt like I was boxing in a library. It was a tricky adjustment to make because I was used to feeding off the crowd and taking their energy, so while I still had the adrenalin for the fight, I did not have the butterflies that an audience would give me. I came up the ramp in my white and gold shorts and gloves, and was surrounded by vacant seats and a total lack of atmosphere. Everyone wore masks apart from me and my opponent. In my corner I was only allowed a couple of members of my team, he the same and then there was the referee. It was so quiet I could hear my opponent's breath and the shots landing. The fight was live on BT Sport, so the thought of that remote audience kept me in the zone, and I still went in with the approach that I was there to knock my opponent out, which I did. I clocked up another win.

I was on a roll, so I went back into training on 1 January 2021 ready for my next lockdown fight, which was on 27 February against Scott Williams at the Copper Box. Again, it was a knockout and another win for me.

On my twenty-second birthday I was in the States with Tyson. He was training and also had some time to relax, so I joined him, and we travelled from Las Vegas to Miami. We trained hard, with some great sparring sessions, and we played hard too: eating, drinking and hanging out by the pool or on the beach. I had an absolute blast for three weeks until I got a phone call from our dad.

'You're fighting on the fifth of June,' he said.

'Er, no I'm not, that's in two weeks' time and I am sat by the pool in Miami, sipping a margarita; what are you talking about?!'

'I got you a fight, you need to get on the first flight home.'

I told Tyson.

'Well, you better go home then. And good luck to you!' He laughed.

Good luck indeed. I got back and did my first training session with Dad. Although I had kept training while I was in the States, I had also been eating and drinking whatever I wanted. I was severely out of shape for someone who had to get in the ring within the fortnight, and Dad and I had words about postponing the fight. He refused to.

'You shouldn't have been living it up,' he said. And he was right. It was a big lesson for me and a reminder that I needed to be on the ball and ready for it. Dad wanted to see what I had in the tank, how I operated when my mind wasn't on the job and if I could cope with last-minute plans. I had to show him that I could.

The fight was at Telford International Centre against Jordan Grant, and it was tough. As well as not being in the best shape, I had also been really ill leading up to the night. It wasn't Covid, but I had a flu bug which sent me to bed for a few days. It was touch and go as to whether I would be well enough to fight, so everyone was relieved when I felt better by Thursday and managed to get back on my feet. I was excited to be boxing in front of a crowd again, even if they were sitting two seats apart from each other. I got the win, in my sparkly black and gold shorts, and it showed I could do it even on a bad night, but it wasn't easy, and I learned a lot from dragging myself through that experience. Sometimes dads do know best, but don't tell my dad that!

After the fight, Tyson put out a rousing message about me on the socials. He shared the viewer ratings of how many people tuned in when I fought, and he said they were higher than world champions. Then he went a step further and called out an American YouTuber turned professional boxer, Jake 'The Problem Child' Paul, saying he should fight me. Tyson was very good at stirring the pot. I didn't even know who Jake was.

7

Problem Child

It was me against depression and I was losing. It felt like I was in the biggest fight of my life without my gloves, a trainer or any sense in my head. I was half asleep in the blue corner while depression came out punching from the red corner. It hit me square in the jaw, intent on a knockout.

There is always a lot of bluster in the lead up to organising a fight, and social media is made for this. Calling someone out is a popular and speedy way to declare an intention and provoke interest without first going through the long round of promoters, managers and lawyers. It leapfrogs this first part of the process, which can often be time-consuming and sends everyone round in circles. It's really very simple. A boxer goes onto their social media accounts and posts a video, throwing down the gauntlet to the person they want to fight. It's an invitation of sorts, played out in front of the whole world rather than behind closed doors. The public nature of it creates an instant impact, a media frenzy, and the momentum continues to play out in front of a global audience. It doesn't mean the fight will definitely go ahead, but it stands a good chance. This is a very different approach from the old days and most of us boxers use it to our advantage.

People call me out all the time, but I don't have time to do the same back, as everyone seems to want to fight me! When I pick up the message, I know instantly whether I want to fight that boxer or not and then we move on to the next stage, which is to set up a call involving the teams on both sides and then dates, money and terms are discussed. Setting up boxing in the traditional way takes so long that sometimes the fights never happen. At least with YouTubers there's a bit of verbal argy bargy which turns into a feud and is then resolved in a big glitzy fight. They get things done. There may be more of a showman element to it, fuelled by hype, marketing and brazen declarations like betting your purse on the outcome or the loser getting a tattoo, but at least it happens.

After Tyson prodded Jake Paul, Jake posted a video in response, asking me why I was getting my brother to call him out.

'If you want to fight,' he said, 'then call me out yourself.'

I thought, Who is this guy from Cleveland, Ohio? Because whoever he is, I am not having this sort of talk. So, I posted a video back saying I didn't need my brother to tell me I was going to fight Jake next because I knew I was. As soon as I saw his message, I knew I wanted to get my hands on him.

The offer came through from his side inviting me to go to America and fight his sparring partner and, if I won, then Jake would agree to fight me. This isn't usual practice, but Jake wasn't a usual boxer, he was a YouTube sensation who had recently turned professional in boxing and things were different in that world. He wanted to see me box before he decided to fight me, and who better to do that with than his sparring partner, because he could get the measure of me pretty fast. It was a control issue and a massive test, but I understood how it worked and I was happy to go along with it.

Jake was headlining a fight in August 2021, and I agreed to fight on the undercard against Anthony Taylor, an ex-MMA fighter who regularly trained with Jake. It was to be my US debut, which was a huge deal, designed to make a big splash and introduce me over there. I couldn't wait. The one massive issue was that because of Dad's criminal record, he wasn't allowed in the country. I was going to miss him as my trainer and as my dad, but there wasn't anything we could do about it. Instead, he worked hard with me throughout my eight weeks of UK training, and he contacted a Mexican guy he knew, Jorge Capetillo, who was a renowned boxing trainer living in Las Vegas and who had worked with Tyson in the past. He told him about the fight, that I didn't know anyone out there or how it all worked, and asked if he could look after me. We did a deal for him to come and join my team, which included Roman, Chris, Andy (my nutritionist) and a couple of others from my usual line-up. Arthur came too, so I was very well supported.

We flew out a week before the fight, in matching Fury tracksuits, picked up a shiny rental SUV and drove to the house which was to be home for the duration of our stay. I think I had accidentally booked something in the ghetto part of Cleveland. The house was nice, classically American with a front stoop, but the cellar was grim and gave me sleepless nights because I have seen too many scary films. It was something else, not helped by a horror movie night after dinner which resulted in us all playing pranks and frightening each other witless.

The next day we picked up food for the week and stocked up on protein, my favourite sort of shopping. I was getting more serious about my diet at this point and Andy was revolutionising my approach with help from his company, Prep by Gainz. Up until now, nutrition had not been my strong point. When I lived at home, Mum and I would occasionally swing by West One Retail Park for a cheeky McDonald's, especially after a big training session or a fight, where my favourite order was two delicious McRibs. I used to eat whatever I could because it was fuel. I didn't care what it was as long as it filled me up. I was so hopeless with my diet I would eat everything and had no understanding of nutrition and empty calories. I may have worked out what I needed to do with my body, but not what to put in it. When I was fifteen it was mostly crap – sweets, biscuits, chocolate – and it kept me going through early mornings, exercise and growth spurts. I would have toast for breakfast, a slice of pizza and a brownie at school, snacks when I got home and then Mum's homecooked dinner. I love my food and back then I thought I could eat anything because I would train it off.

It was a revelation when I began to understand that what I ate would help my body to train longer and better. I now work with a dietician and nutritionist, and I always have someone with me during training camps to prepare my meals, which makes the world of difference. It's about feeling the best I can, every single day. Everything is dialled in now and it is a completely different approach from my previous chaos of training and winning without a proper plan. Camp life is tightly scheduled – what and when to eat, when to sleep and for how long, and when to train – which is a real safety net for me. My American fight was the first time I had put these new habits into practice.

Monday morning started with a training session to get a light sweat on and keep me loosened up and then Jorge the trainer came over on Tuesday to put me through my paces and work out on the pads. Although his English was good, he had a heavy accent and I found it hard to understand what he was saying. I was not sure how it would work when we were in the ring, with the noise of the crowd and me trying to listen to instruction. But I had done the training, so I felt reassured that I would be able to get myself through it whatever.

Fight week is different in the States – it's bigger and better with lots of TV coverage, live interviews, famous announcers like Jimmy Lennon Jr and more fuss made leading up to the main event. Wednesday was the public workout and a chance for everyone to watch us shadow box, check out what sort of shape we were in and build the anticipation for Saturday night. Then the press conference was Thursday. It was great to thank everyone for having me and say that while they knew who my brother Tyson was, they would soon know me too and I brought my own game. Saturday was crunch time. After ten weeks of training and careful diet, I needed to be on weight. We went from the official weigh-in to the public one, where I hit 12st 11lbs, so I was spot on and it kicked off a little bit with Anthony Taylor, my opponent, as is usual. That night we went to an Italian restaurant and I loaded up on carbs. All the training, talking, media and build-up was done. It was all over bar the fighting.

Just before the fight, I warmed up on the pads in the changing room with Jorge. I was feeling fantastic, and I was wearing my stars and stripes Apollo Creed shorts with gold gloves and a blue robe with both the GB and USA flags on. Remember my six-year-old self at Christmas? If only he could have seen me in that moment! The noise from the spectators was intense as I walked out; it was like being back in Manchester. I took a few deep breaths to remind myself I was in one of my favourite countries in the world and I wallowed in the atmosphere before I stepped into the ring. Right, let's do this.

I met my opponent in the middle of the ring, our chests pressed against each other. I was a few significant inches taller and when I looked at him, all I saw in that moment was a scared, weak man. The referee, George Nichols, came up close and his voice rang out loud and clear: 'Boxers, you have previously been given your instructions. Obey my commands at all times. Protect yourself at all times. With love, touch 'em up, guys.' We tapped gloves.

I came out bouncing, my golden gloves flashing under the ring spotlights. On the front foot, I led with a few left-handed jabs before throwing a couple of good right hands in. I was keeping the space between us, feeling light and powerful and nailing some big shots, before his head went down and he rammed me against the ropes. I wasn't worried. My next right hand caught him, and I could see him falter. He looked a bit dazed, like he couldn't quite focus on where I was. The bell rang and I went back to my corner. Jorge was there with water and wise words.

'Everything is beautiful. Keep your hands up. He is coming at you from the top.' I nodded. My opponent was already on his feet, pacing, seemingly impatient to continue or get it over with.

In the second of four rounds I landed a left hook I was happy with and went for a succession of blows, getting into a good rhythm. I was in control, and I felt my opponent's mood shift. He didn't seem to want to fight, he wasn't engaging, he was just taking every opportunity to come in for a hug and hang off my neck. The crowd didn't appreciate it either and there was some booing. I was still moving as he bent double, out of breath and stretching the seconds. We picked up the pace again and a couple of swings later he had fallen against me and almost into the ropes, managing to pull himself out just in time.

Yet again, he was out in the ring for the third round way before the bell went. Maybe his mum had his tea on the table: he seemed in a big hurry to continue and yet he wasn't getting many good shots in. I was happy with my technique, but I could imagine it wasn't a great watch. At one point he was tucked under my left armpit and as I pulled myself away, he almost went back through the ropes again. This was not what I was used to or had been expecting. A minute later, he tripped over his own feet, went down on all fours and almost left the ring completely.

Then it was the last round of my big USA debut. I knew Jake Paul and his brother Logan would be watching and considering a fight. Dad's words to me played on a loop in my head: 'Rely on your boxing smarts.' I gave a volley of big body shots before my opponent clung to me again. What was it with this guy? His right hand swung out but didn't make contact as my right hand connected. In the closing seconds, he fell into me and for a third time his head went through the ropes as the crowd booed in response to what was a disappointing end to a frustrating fight.

Jimmy Lennon Jr was in the ring ready to declare the winner.

'Ladies and gentlemen, after four rounds of action the judges are in agreement, and we have a unanimous decision. All three judges scored about the same, forty to thirty-six, all three in favour of the winner . . . and still undefeated . . . Tommy "TNT" Furrrrryyyy.' While I may have raised my arms in the air and then gone to the corner of the ring to stand on the ropes and thank the crowd, it was a pretty low-key celebration for me. I felt an acute sense of disappointment.

Look, I know I am my own worst critic, and can be pretty hard on myself, but the fight didn't go how I wanted it to. My opponent just wanted to hold and smother, which in boxing terms makes it no fun to watch. I didn't feel like I got enough good shots. It was scrappy and hard on the eye. Yes, I won, but it wasn't what I imagined it would be. I had come out with a vision in my mind of a big spectacular, a stylish fight, and it didn't come anywhere close to that. I am not a perfectionist because I don't believe perfection exists – I'm realistic. That said, I just want to be the best I can be and, as a successful boxer, I don't think you can be any other way. I can find criticism in anything, whether it's in my training, my fights or the way I look, although I am trying to cut myself some slack as I get older. Afterwards I was very upset and shed a few tears. I rang Dad and said I thought it was a wasted opportunity. He knew exactly what to say.

'That's boxing,' he said, from what felt like a million miles away back in the UK, 'you will get those people who hang on to you, he won't be the last, you won every round so just enjoy that.'

He was right. A win was still a win. After that conversation I could move on, but what about Jake Paul and his agreement to face me in the ring if I beat his sparring partner? After my fight, I was in the corridor giving an interview to BT Sport and Jake had just finished too. The interviewer spotted him before I did and craftily grabbed him to ask if he had any words for me, so suddenly we were up in each other's faces. He was loud and arrogant.

'You need to stop running, my friend,' I said and then there was a bit of a scuffle with some of our team. As we were separated, I shouted over to him, 'Take the fight! Take the fight!'

After the drama of that moment, my team and I went to a party thrown by another undercard, Montana Love, in a local club, but I wasn't in the mood to drink and socialise, and was happiest when we went back to the rental house for pizza.

I woke up the following morning feeling down. It

had been a massive anti-climax and it was really affecting my mood. We were only a short flight away
from LA, so why not add some fun on to the trip?
Everyone else had to head home, but Chris was up for
coming with me and so we spent a few days staying
in a great hotel and going to Universal Studios, which
perked me right up.

When I got back, I started training again as Jake
Paul had confirmed he wanted to fight. Maybe he
wouldn't have done if I had knocked out his sparring
partner, so what I'd hated about that fight had done
me a favour in the long run. Perhaps I wasn't perceived
as a big threat. Well, big mistake! Dad and Frank
Warren worked together with the lawyers behind
closed doors to set up a fight between me and Jake.
There was a lot riding on this as he was a successful
YouTuber, infamous for his controversial pranks,
music career as a rapper and undefeated boxing
record, and I was a professional boxer and the brother
of the heavyweight champion of the world. We both
had a lot to lose, but I had more at stake within the
sports world. The contracts were finally agreed, we
went on to social media to make the announcement
and declarations of when, where and how much we
would weigh, following the usual process. It was a
highly anticipated clash with a lot of global interest
and was billed as a mega fight. The countdown began.

Luckily, Tyson didn't have any immediate commitments after his fight against Deontay Wilder in October, where he had retained his WBC heavyweight title, so he trained me alongside Dad. We did the training camp at Tyson's gym at his house in Morecambe and I was there full time. Everything was on track for the fight on 18 December 2021.

We were four weeks in, and I was battling a horrible bacterial infection, but otherwise it was going really well. One morning, I was on the pads and then working with a guy wearing a body bag. As I threw a shot, he threw one back and it caught the side of my torso. It was only meant to be a check shot but this guy, who was a friend of Tyson's, was seventeen stone and had no gloves on, so he was only supposed to be touching certain places. I was weakened by the illness, and we must have connected wrong because all of a sudden I felt the weight of his punch and the breath left my body. I didn't feel right for a few seconds and then I was OK again, so we moved on to core work. I was sat in a crunch position while Dad tapped my stomach, left side, right side and then middle with a ten-kilo ball. He smashed thirty hits on the middle, but on the twenty-fifth hit on my left, that side of my body shut down. I was hunched over and I couldn't breathe. I had never experienced pain like it before, and I don't mind telling you, I thought I was going to die.

It was crippling to breathe normally and I resorted to shallow breaths. I couldn't speak, so everyone knew it was serious and we went straight to hospital. The MRI scan and specialist told us what we already knew – I had broken two ribs and they had snapped clean in half, like twigs. This was a couple of weeks before my flight to Tampa, Florida for the Jake Paul fight. There was no way my ribs would heal in time. I was in a state of shock.

My whole world felt apart. I was this kid from Salford with no money and a big dream. I may have done well financially after coming out of *Love Island*, but the fee I would have earned on this fight was something else. This was the big time. All of a sudden it was whipped away and I was looking at no fight, lost income and months of recovery. To have it taken away from me by somebody else was a pill I couldn't swallow at the time, and I thought the opportunity would never come round again.

I left Morecambe and went back to Manchester. I didn't think things could get much worse, but once the news of the fight cancellation hit the press, everything kicked off. I received a torrent of online abuse, my accusers saying I was 'scared of a YouTuber', 'not a Fury', 'a fake fighter', 'embarrassing my family' and much worse. Every single day there were more messages coming through saying unimaginable stuff that

I really don't want to repeat here. It was relentless and the press joined in too. I came off social media and I rarely went out in public because I would get heckled in the street.

When I did leave the house, all of those things would be said in person, to my face. I'm not sure how people have the audacity to do this, but they do. While it was a red rag to a bull, there was nothing I could do about it. I couldn't react because I didn't want them to see how much it hurt, and I certainly couldn't go around hitting people because I would end up behind bars. And this is where I do rate myself and my maturity level because I was barely in my twenties and it would have been easy to retaliate, yet in those situations, I remained calm, composed and tipped my cap to anyone having a go at me. I didn't rise to it, and I was able to quell all the rage, anger and fight inside me and hang on to my sanity for dear life. I found something within that enabled me to take no notice. I surprised myself because I didn't know I had it in me, but thank the Lord I do, and it has enabled me to keep out of trouble. Regardless of the level of abuse I received and my background as a Fury and a boxer, I held my head high and turned away.

It was upsetting and also frustrating because nobody had wanted this fight more than me and people were assuming I had pulled out because I was afraid. That hurt the most. I released the medical report so everyone knew I was injured, but by then the damage was done and I sank into a low mood I couldn't shake myself out of. Of course, I would have my down days, but I had never felt like this before. It was a really dark few weeks, and I was not good to live with; Molly couldn't console me. I also couldn't exercise until my ribs had healed, which really didn't help. When I did go out, it was to bars nobody went to and I drank to dull the pain, not for fun.

There was no motivation to do anything. I was going through the motions, but I wasn't present, and I had no interest in looking after myself. I knew I was spiralling, and I wasn't bothered – I just didn't care. I was down on everything, even thinking that maybe being a sportsman was a shit career and that boxing was making me unhappy. This wasn't true, but I couldn't talk myself round. It was the bleakest, toughest time I had experienced.

Molly noticed the change in me, of course, and didn't know what to do because she had never seen me like this before. My mood affected her deeply and she was at a loss as to how to reach me. One day she came home with food she knew I liked, and it didn't do anything, it didn't hit the spot. This was really unlike me because I love my food and it's usually guaranteed to cheer me up.

'What can I do?' Molly asked. 'I don't know how to help. How can I help you to pull yourself out of this?' She was desperate to make it all OK.

'There's nothing you can do. Nothing means anything to me anymore and I can't help it, this is just the way I feel.' That was the truth in that moment.

'What do you mean by that?' I know Molly was struggling to understand how the situation had unravelled and affected me so severely. Surely it was just a frustrating injury and a cancelled fight at the end of the day? She didn't say this out loud, but I suspected that was what she was thinking because that was what I was beating myself up with. How had I let it floor me?

'I feel like everything has been taken away from me.' I just wanted to sit in the house and look out of the window, drinking and eating rubbish. This was so hard for Molly to hear, but she didn't give up on me. Over the days and weeks that followed, she kept trying to talk to me, and as I opened up about the situation it really helped. I couldn't access my emotions easily or admit that I was depressed, but I did talk a bit and the support I received from Molly, my family and friends was invaluable. It began to alleviate how I was feeling. I would encourage anyone struggling with their mental health to tell someone. Ask for help. If you can, talk to one or several people close to you. In hindsight, I probably should have sought a professional ear too. Of course, we rely on the people we love, but sometimes it's hard to share stuff because we don't want to worry those closest to us.

It was a shock to have found myself in this position and the turning point came when my ribs started to heal and I was allowed to begin training again. As quickly as I had sunk, I began to rise. Feeling the care of everyone around me and being able to exercise was a game changer. I started with a little run, which led to doing a few weights, which led to getting back in the boxing gym for pads and circuits, before eventually I was back sparring. I felt like myself for the first time in many weeks. Progress was slow but steady and I was ecstatic to be back in training. I thought it was just a mental health blip, the result of a disappointment and lack of exercise. I was sure I wouldn't get caught out again. How wrong I was.

But it was now spring, and I had just had a productive session in the gym as I built myself back up. I was whistling on the way home and feeling good – just general happiness, not about anything in particular. I came through the door with a protein shake in my hand and immediately sensed that the energy was different. I could hear a pin drop and that is not normal in our house: usually stuff is going on and there are people around. It was the middle of the day, and I thought this was strange, and then I saw Molly sitting in the kitchen, not on her phone. Even stranger.

'All right, babe, is everything OK?' I thought I was in trouble – I think that is my default setting – but I couldn't think what for, so I tried a smile to test the waters.

'Come and sit down.' Molly smiled back, so that must mean I wasn't in that much trouble. I sat down and Molly handed me a small box.

'Got you a little present. Open it,' she said. There was something going on here that I couldn't put my finger on. I thought it might be a T-shirt, a belt or maybe some jewellery although I couldn't think of an anniversary or a reason for it. I opened the gift and inside was a tiny Babygro with an elephant on it, signifying our 'parenting' of her cuddly toy Elly Belly. It took a few seconds for this to register, and I looked up at Molly who had the biggest smile. I did a double take. Surely she wasn't telling me what I thought she was telling me?!

'No, there's no way, please do not be joking with me,' I said, thinking this sort of prank was not her style. She showed me the pregnancy test. I was in complete shock. I'd had no inkling that this was in store for us; the idea of Molly being pregnant was furthest from my mind, even though we did not take precautions and had talked about having a baby. We were ready and happy with whatever happened whenever it did, and it turned out to be right now. I pulled Molly onto my lap and we were euphoric. We couldn't wait for what was to come. I was going to be a daddy. In that moment my entire world shifted on its axis, just as it had done when I came out of *Love Island*.

In the meantime, I needed to get back in the ring. Tyson had seen me dip and he was instrumental in setting up my next fight. I thought I had lost the opportunity with Jake Paul and my big money day had gone, so I just needed to get back out there and do what I did. Tyson was headlining a fight at Wembley Stadium on 23 April 2022, and I was there on the undercard, which was the first time we had ever fought in the same event. It would also be my first fight back after my injury, so I had a lot to prove to myself.

Arriving at Wembley was mad because it was sold out, meaning more than 94,000 people were making their way to the stadium so the traffic was at a standstill and I nearly missed my own fight. When I finally got there, I had half an hour to wrap my hands, change, go through my rituals and get in the zone, which wasn't the best start, but I had a good warm-up and there were great vibes in the changing room. Dad was excited that we were on the same bill. I think this is still one of the best boxing memories he has, seeing two of his boys fight at Wembley, one in the main event and the other as an undercard.

I remember standing in the tunnel, in my black robe, and as I walked out, I was hit by how massive the place was; I couldn't believe this was really happening. It was another pinch-me moment and it reminded me, at exactly the moment I needed it, that this was what I was born to do. It was a big tick in the career box, and I was in my element for the ring walk. Hello, Wembley!

I fought Daniel Bocianski and let me tell you, that man is a machine. I was hitting him with some good shots, and I knocked him down in the fifth round, but he managed to get back up with a bad cut over his eye, blood pumping out of him. I still have my shorts from that fight, covered in his blood. Dad thought the referee should have stopped the fight in my favour. Instead, it went to points and I won by unanimous decision.

I stayed to cheer on Tyson, who was defending his heavyweight championship of the world. It was a massive fight and he put in an unbelievable performance with a knockout in the sixth round. To be honest, I have never found it easy watching my brothers in the ring. It is horrible. I believe in them and their ability, but the fight is out of my hands, and I have no control over the way it's going to go. Part of me wants to be in the ring instead and the other part of me just wants to protect them. I am on the edge of my seat all the time, it is anxiety on steroids; I can't sit still, and my heart is thumping. By the end of the fight, I'm almost as tired as if I have been in the ring myself. It is not a nice feeling, but they do the same for me, so I am there for them. It is a bit like sitting in the passenger seat of the car and wanting to be at the wheel. If they were football players it would be different, because nine times out of ten they would be safe, but both my brothers are heavyweights, so one shot, one wayward punch, and I could be talking to a different person for the rest of my life. It is a serious game. I know they are just as worried about me. Of course, I don't think about this when I step into the ring. I am in a totally different mindset, prepared to die in that moment because all I want is the win. I'm not thinking logically. I thank God for every day that we are all alive and well.

That night was one of the best memories for me as an individual and for us as a family; there was no way it could have gone any better. We left the stadium, stopped off at the petrol station to buy beer and sweets, and then went back to the house we had rented for the week. We must have stayed up until 4 a.m. talking over both fights. It had been so special to be there alongside my brother, the man who put our name in international lights and think that maybe I could do that one day too.

After that fight, Jake Paul's manager got in touch,

and he said they still wanted to do the fight. So I had a new date, 6 August, to work towards and a training camp scheduled. Contracts were finalised and Madison Square Garden – a dream of a location – was booked, a venue ten times bigger than the first one, and it sold out fast. It appeared that the delay after the previous cancellation had only made people more interested. My broken ribs and dark mood were a distant memory, and I even began to think this had all been in my favour. Can you see where this is heading?

I had to go to New York for the press conference several weeks before the fight. I was fighting fit and super excited as I boarded the train to the airport with my team, all of us in matching tracksuits as usual. We got to the airport in good time and were about to go through customs when a security guy came over and asked if I could go with him for a second. This hadn't happened before, but I wasn't unduly worried.

'You know you are not travelling anywhere today, don't you?' he said.

'Sorry? What do you mean?' I wondered if this was a wind-up and if so, it wasn't very funny because our plane was on the tarmac, and we were not on it.

'Yeah, you aren't going anywhere, your ESTA and visa have been cancelled.' He wasn't joking.

'Mate, I don't really understand what's going on,' I said calmly, 'but I have a very big fight coming up in

New York in six weeks and I am going over for the press conference. There must be some mistake. They are expecting me there.' We were all in matching tracksuits for goodness' sake.

'No, there is not going to be a fight, you have been denied access to the US for this moment in time.'

My stomach dropped lower than I thought possible. The first fight had been cancelled, which had resulted in everybody and their mum calling me a coward, a shithouse, not a real boxer, an embarrassment to my family and all the names under the sun. Nobody really believed why I had pulled out of my first fight, even after I put the doctor's report out there. So, imagine the residual heat from that situation, and now I was being told my second fight was in jeopardy. I could not cancel again. We were in total shock; I couldn't believe it and I called my lawyer from the airport. I told him I didn't know what had gone wrong, but we needed to jump on it quickly or risk a second fight cancellation, which I couldn't deal with. We had to resolve the issue as soon as possible or I might spontaneously combust.

It turned out to be a problem that couldn't be sorted out straight away, involving total confusion around my last name. It had nothing to do with me and it has now been resolved, and my name cleared, but it was obvious that my lawyer would have to set to it. I left the airport when we realised it would take days rather than hours to negotiate. We had to make up a story to get me out of the press conference, a little white lie as to why I couldn't get there, in the hope that this was a tiny blip that would be quickly rectified. I laid low for a week or so while my lawyer worked tirelessly. When I got the call saying I still couldn't get into the US and the fight would have to be cancelled, I couldn't believe it. After a second round of hype, expectation and hard graft, it was over before it had begun.

I had to come out and say sorry for the second time and explain that I couldn't get into the country, let alone the ring, and there was nothing I could do about it. It was mortifying; apart from anything else I was so embarrassed. How was I back in the same position again? Imagine the storm of internet abuse and self-loathing I struggled with first time around and then make it twice as heavy. At least the first fight was called off because I had a physical injury – this time it didn't make sense to anyone, least of all me. The stick I received for pulling out again was completely out of proportion, but I carried it around with me and used it to beat myself with. It was completely out of my control. I had been denied access by the government; it was an impossible situation which had nothing to do with me, and there wasn't a single thing I could do to change it.

In the middle of the night, I would wake up thinking

maybe there was a reason why this had happened again? Perhaps God was telling me that something wasn't right, that it wasn't meant to be. I thought the fight was cursed. It would be forever known as The Fight that Never Happened. My chance of earning serious money was gone and this time around it was harder to take because we had a baby on the way. All I wanted was to provide for my family. I was in a complete state; everything was crumbling around me. I tried to hold on to normal life, but I would walk down the street to get a coffee only for people to stop in their cars, wind the window down and shout abuse at me. I was being heckled in public and I didn't want to go out just for people to tell me how shit I was to my face. I'm not looking for sympathy, but can you imagine that? It is the strangest, most unsettling position to be in when strangers come up to you just to be rude or take the time to write unkind comments online. This had started when the first fight was cancelled and there was no let-up: now they had even more reason to verbally attack me. As I had done before, I kept my head in public. In private I was a mess.

I have always been quite thick skinned, particularly where other people's opinions about me are concerned, but the cancellations and the response to them took me down. Every time I posted on Instagram there were awful messages in the comments below. I was fair game. I was still doing brand stuff and weirdly my follower numbers rose, as people were fascinated by the drama that was being played out. I was arguing with Molly and couldn't be the nice, caring loving guy that I really am. I had disappeared into myself at the time she needed me most.

It was me against depression and I was losing. It felt like I was in the biggest fight of my life without my gloves, a trainer or any sense in my head. I was half asleep in the blue corner while depression came out punching from the red corner. It hit me square in the jaw, intent on a knockout. I was powerless in the face of the booze, crap food, late nights, lack of exercise and self-hatred it was throwing in my direction. It had me on the ropes and I didn't care. I knew I was doing all the stuff that made me feel worse about myself and I couldn't get a sure footing in reality for what felt like forever, but was more like a couple of months. I was fully expecting depression to reign victorious in the ring, its arm raised in triumph while I slumped onto the canvas, a bloody, bloated mess.

So how did I turn that fight around and take depression down? There was no magic moment, just a growing realisation that I was at the very rocky bottom of things, and I couldn't continue to treat myself so badly. I took a long look in the mirror. I was severely overweight and out of shape. I had let myself go and I had to say out loud to my reflection, 'This can't continue.' I repeated the quote Dad would say to me, which has stuck with me my whole life and ultimately brought me out of everything: 'What's for you in life won't pass you by.'

I rammed it into my skull. I thought, God has already made a plan for me; instead of worrying about stuff, I just needed to trust in what was ahead. And I repeated Tyson's old adage that there is no use crying over spilled milk. If it's meant to be it will happen, and if not then that's that. It's done. Once I stopped caring so deeply about the situation, everything got better for me. My usual approach to life is that one door closes and another one opens, and yet I had forgotten or chosen to ignore this. Slowly, I began to pull myself out of my pit of despair. I looked around at what I had. A beautiful girlfriend, a longed-for baby on the way, a comfortable home and some money in the bank. At my lowest points, I felt worthless and I couldn't see the positives clearly, but now I could, and I knew how much I had to lose.

I am well aware how many people battle with mental health issues, and everyone's experience of them is very personal. My situation is no reflection or judgement on anyone else and I know how lucky I was. Yes, I did pull myself out of it twice, but it isn't always possible to do this on your own and professional support is often the answer. I wanted to share my story to show how this can happen to anyone, in small yet significant ways, and that there is always light at the end of the tunnel. I am not here to be a spokesperson or imagine that I understand what others go through; I just want to add my voice and experience. If it is helpful to one other person to hear this, then it is well worth me writing about what I went through.

Maybe what happened to me could be better described as being temporarily blind-sided by an overwhelming hopelessness. I don't think there is a word for that. I think I can say I was depressed, and I doubt that will be the last time I feel like that, but I wouldn't say I suffer with depression. That's a very different thing. It takes many guises – just look at my brother Tyson, who has had his own public struggle with mental health issues. I don't want to speak too much for him because he has already openly shared his battles and diagnoses in an articulate, brave and powerful way. I was still a teen when Tyson was going through addiction and depression. I was too young to really understand how to communicate with him or find a way to help, but I knew what the problems were, and I kept in close touch with him, always being upbeat and talking about anything other than boxing. I do remember thinking that if our dad can't get through to him, what difference could I make, but the trick is to keep talking and trying.

I know one of the catalysts for Tyson's recovery – other than his lovely wife, Paris, and their brilliant kids – was the day he went out for a short run and had to give up, walking the rest of the way. It was then that he knew he had to get fit and healthy again. I am really proud of how he has dealt with it all, and seeing him overcome such hurdles has helped me when I faced my own difficulties.

When I was feeling really low, it was the weirdest experience, like being stuck behind a sheet of glass and watching everything going on around me, but not being able to be truly part of it. The world moved from Technicolor to grey. Life was passing me by, and I was letting it. As someone who lives to box, there was no fight in me.

Unsurprisingly, like Tyson, exercise works for me too and going to the gym is our safe haven. If I am having a shitty day, I go for a three-mile run, have a protein shake and it makes me feel so much better. When I was at training camp, I had a big bathtub in the gym with the water at three degrees and I would get up at 6 a.m. and sit in it for three minutes before I did anything else. The endorphins lasted all day. I swear by a routine. It is why I enjoy the camps, even if they are an absolute slog, because I thrive in the structure of a well-thought-out schedule of boxing sessions, sleep, exercise and healthy eating. By the end of it I feel like a fully functioning machine and believe there is nothing in the world I can't conquer. This is such an addictive state of mind, but in a good way.

I know it's hard to get motivated when all you want to do is go to bed and curl up under the duvet, but I promise you just half an hour of activity every day really works and, while this won't be news to anyone, I do think we all need reminding, me included. I am not suggesting you start lifting weights or pummelling a punch bag (unless that's what you enjoy), but you should find something you can do regularly that is appropriate for you and fits in with your life.

You don't have to be a boxer or a professional athlete to set up your own 'training camp' either. Give it a go and start with a short-term goal of sticking to the schedule for seven or fourteen days. Maybe go out each morning for a twenty-minute run or an interval training combination of running and walking. Alternatively, a brisk forty-minute walk for a breath of fresh air, to get the blood pumping and be out in the light, can give a new perspective on things and a clarity you may have been missing.

Swimming isn't top of my list, but it is one of the best ways of exercising, so head down to your local leisure centre or, if you are lucky enough to be near the sea, a river or lake, then go one step further into the incredible world of wild swimming. Be careful: make sure the body of water you are getting into is safe, designated for swimming and that you understand the tides, currents, depths and know an easy exit. If you are a beginner, pace yourself and build up to full immersion in cold water, listening to the way your body responds to the temperature, and don't get into the water alone. There are brilliant outdoor swimming websites full of advice, so do your research before you take the plunge. Cold-water therapy is very fashionable at the moment, and I can vouch for the incredible dopamine hit it gives, but do not be fooled into thinking you can just get in to freezing water without any sort of preparation. You can also turn your morning shower gradually colder for the final minute or so for similar benefits.

It isn't just about exercise, but also about what we eat. A bowl of porridge with fruit and honey is one of the most nutritious breakfast choices, and carrying a refillable bottle helps you stay hydrated and keeps track of how much you are drinking. This, coupled with exercise, gives you the best start to the day and helps you stay on track. Don't pile on the pressure for this to be the 'new you', because it's easy to get bored and abandon it, but after a week or two you should begin to notice a difference in your general wellbeing.

So why not extend it for another week? Maybe add ten more minutes to your run or walk and another minute to your cold shower. Factor in treats, to stop yourself giving up too soon; it works for me. You may want to consider other parts of your day and look at healthy meal planning, more exercise and getting a good night's sleep. Don't try to fix everything at once, but adopting a couple of practices and repeating them can quickly become a happy habit.

To help lift my mood after the second Jake Paul fight cancellation, I signed up for a triathlon. I had a few weeks to prepare so I went out and bought a bike. The same day, I did a 5k run and a twelve-mile cycle and I thought, OK I can do this, although I knew the swim would be my weak point. That's not my natural place and I struggled with it during the training. I went to Yorkshire for the triathlon, and it was an interesting experience with great people. The swim was indeed the hardest part of it all, but I am glad I pushed myself out of my comfort zone. It shook everything up in the best way. A triathlon would never replace the commitment I had to training and boxing, but it gave me a target to aim for and a reason to stay on track. I was ready for whatever was next.

After *Love Island*, even boxing trainers said to me I would be a fool to go back into boxing, and that I was better off earning my money through brand deals and avoiding a broken nose, but that wasn't how it worked for me. I knew if I did that my life would have no real purpose or goals. The thought of a fight ahead gets me moving. It all stems back to being a child, with the determination, commitment and sacrifice I carried, and all those moments flooded back to me when I was having a tough time. I had worked too hard and put too much into my boxing career just to let it go after a couple of setbacks. With support from Molly, my family and friends, I was determined to come back better than ever, and that was the final push I needed. I wanted another fight to prepare for.

My next fight was unusual in that I had a camera crew following me around in the lead up to it. Molly and I had agreed to feature in Paris and Tyson's multi-part Netflix documentary *At Home with the Furys*, which followed Tyson's early days of retirement from boxing. It was a fly-on-the-wall-style series which focused on their lives over six months or so, showing them as parents, partners and professionals and my dad had a nice part in it too. Tyson asked Molly and me if we were up for taking part and we were happy to. We were used to being filmed – after all that's how we met – and we were comfortable doing pieces to camera. It was also a special time for us to document because we had not yet announced Molly's pregnancy so, before we did, we met up with Tyson, Paris and the kids for some food and to tell them the happy news. They could not have been more thrilled for us. Tyson jumped up and hugged me, ruffling my hair like the big brother he is, and Paris threw her arms around Molly. The moment called for a champagne toast and I am forever grateful it was caught on camera in the series.

Molly and I weren't heavily involved in the programme, it only required us for a few days here and there and the crew were brilliant to have around. We had a great experience filming, and the series captured our lives really well; nothing was done for the cameras and what you see is exactly who we all are. The show was predominantly about Tyson and Paris, and Molly and I enjoyed being a small part of it. My story in the show culminated in my eighth professional fight, which took place in Dubai, and I was happy to have the production team coming there with me to give an insight into the build-up, as well as following my training at home.

I was scheduled to fight the American Paul Bamba on 13 November 2022 in Dubai, which was a welcome plan after my last fight at Wembley in April and the trauma of the second Jake Paul cancellation. Tyson was booked to fight Derek Chisora III the following month, so it made sense to set up a training camp together. It meant we were away from all the distractions; we could get into the right mindset and stay in it for as long as possible. When I arrived at our Fury Camp House with Dad, we were met by Tyson, standing on the staircase wearing a dressing gown and a bowler hat. Dad jumped out of his skin and outwardly groaned when Tyson summoned us to the front room for a conference. I inwardly groaned because even though a training camp with him is one of the funniest things you can imagine, Tyson has a set of ground rules he lives by, and he told us if we didn't abide by them then we couldn't stay. These included no shoes beyond the porch, and he showed us how to plump the cushions once we had got up from the chair. The camera crew filmed this and I knew they were loving it!

Preparing to train for a fight alongside Tyson was amazing. We smashed out session after session in the gym and he pushed me further than I had ever been and also made me want to be around him. There is only one Tyson.

'I am not trying to live up to him or step in his boots, I wanted to step in my own boots, the best boots that I could and be the best boxer I could be,' I said on camera.

Molly was heavily pregnant, and everything was about to change. I had to keep my distance in camp and focus on the job in hand because if my mind wandered it would cost me dear. I needed a win and then I had a week's holiday booked with Molly after the fight and the countdown to our baby's arrival. We had recently found out we were having a little girl! I know Dad was worried about my focus in training camp.

'How are you feeling about impending fatherhood?' he asked; the camera caught our conversation.

'It feels good,' I said. 'It's what life is all about, having a family of my own and it not being about me anymore.' My vision of what I was fighting for had changed. In the past I was fighting for me, fighting to get somewhere, for money, for a bit of respect, a bit of pride. Now I was interested in fighting for my daughter, for Molly, for however many kids we ended up having and to create a secure future for them.

All the hard training work had been done and I was off to Dubai to get Paul Bamba dealt with. The feeling once camp was complete was like no other, particularly because Dubai is one of my favourite holiday destinations, so I was really excited to box over there. I felt relaxed and calm, even though deep down I knew that everything was on the line on Saturday.

Two days before the fight I got on the scales with 4lbs to lose, needing to come down to 12st 12lbs. I wasn't nervous because I normally have to lose 6lbs in the week of the fight and I had done it seven times before. It's one of the things I pride myself on. Dad and I are very professional and believe in doing things right or not doing them at all. The official weigh-in was at 8 a.m. the day before the fight. I knew if I didn't hit my target weight then I would not be fighting.

Molly had arrived by then, bringing my kit out with her. She designs all my boxing kits and I give her a very basic brief which she then runs with and creates mind-blowing outfits. This time around I wanted a silver and white colour theme, but the rest was up to her. I always feel quicker in white; in black gloves I can feel like I am stuck in the mud for some weird reason. I loved what she had come up with. As well as 'FURY' on the front of the waistband she had included 'BABY GIRL' on the back, a little reminder of what was to come and so she could be with me. I also had a long white robe with 'FURY' running around the edging, silver cuffs and my good luck charm of the embroidered Elly Belly elephant on the belt. It was perfect.

It was a privilege to have Molly there with me and Dad could see the twinkle in my eye when she arrived; he knows how good she is for me. He is really fond of her and she of him. All my family love Molly and welcomed her immediately, even though, like my mum, she does not come from a Traveller family. She has even learned a few Traveller words – including 'gorger', the word for a non-Traveller – she doesn't always use them in the right context, but it's a lovely way to connect with Dad.

Weigh-in day dawned and I was feeling great. After a hard training camp, I wanted to show Dad the training had paid off and to put on a good show. Bamba weighed in first and then I got on the scales. I had hit weight and was thrilled, saying the fight was going to be dynamite tomorrow. Then something unexpected happened: Bamba accused me of being seven pounds overweight and he and his team kicked off, saying he didn't want to fight. He also called me unprofessional for not making weight, an insult I took to heart after spending my entire life working hard. It turned out my contract said one thing and his said another and suddenly everything was up in the air. It wasn't looking good, and I had to keep my composure while it got sorted out. I had been here before, but this was the last thing I needed after the year I'd had, particularly while the camera crew were following us around. They needed the fight to happen as much as I did.

As always in these situations, Dad was calm.

'Just sit tight and wait for it to be sorted out. You have done what was stipulated in your contract.' I was dead on the weight and also absolutely starving, so I didn't know whether to eat or not. By the evening, it was confirmed that Bamba had refused to fight because of the weight issue, but I was there and ready, so at the eleventh hour we had to sort out a replacement, who turned out to be a guy around a stone and a half heavier than me and much more experienced. It wasn't ideal but Rolly Lambert was the saviour of the event and willing to step in with only a few hours to go, although it couldn't be sanctioned as a fight. It turned into an exhibition, which was fine by me because without this option, the last two months would have been totally wasted and Netflix would have a whole load of training footage with no fight at the end of it.

Even though it now meant, as an exhibition, there was no winner or loser, I still had to do my job. I had to take punches to my face, and I was not prepared to go down. For Molly, it didn't matter whether it was a real fight or not, it was still dangerous. Besides, by round three it's a real fight anyway, because nobody wants to look bad. I certainly didn't.

In the changing room, I went through the same routine I always do, and Dad led the team prayer, as he always does.

'Lord, let no injuries occur, it's a sport at the end of the day and both boys need to have fun and entertain the crowd. In the name of Jesus, let both men be safe and good luck to both. Amen.'

Amen indeed. We all clapped and then it was showtime.

I paused for a moment before walking out into the

ring. I had to get in the right head space and then I went for it. I could see Molly in the front row, looking fixedly at the floor. I knew how nervous she was for me, and her emotions were heightened because of the pregnancy hormones. And then there was my arch nemesis, Jake Paul, who was commentating on the night, which was a strange decision because he was always going to be negative and rude about me. I didn't know the organisers had flown him out to do the ringside commentating.

The fight began and so did the sneering report from Jake.

'He thinks he's his brother!'

'He's just an Instagram model.'

'You fucking suck, Tommy!'

'You are an amateur still, this is embarrassing!'

As Jake continued to hurl abuse, it made me fight harder. I was determined to show him and everyone else that I deserved to be in the ring because of who I was, not who I was related to.

At the end, after six rounds, Rolly and I hugged. I had more than held my own. If this had been a fight, I would have won on points. Dad was proud of me, and I was proud of myself for having the balls to get in a ring with a fighter with WBC and WBH titles to his name. Then I turned my attention to Jake Paul. That's when it all kicked off.

I was demanding Jake get into the ring with me; he was calling me a pussy and saying Dad was a fat, miserable old man. This was like tipping petrol onto the flames and the red mist came down for Dad; he ripped off his T-shirt like the Incredible Hulk and called Jake into the ring. We were all held back from each other with one of the commentators saying it had 'unfolded terribly, folks'. It was high drama, and it reignited the possibility of a fight with Jake. We both knew we were building to a showdown.

Back in the changing room, I was reunited with Molly who was relieved it was over. Other than taking a blow to the head and sporting a massive lump, I was so happy. Now we could enjoy our babymoon.

The following morning, I woke up to the breakfast of champions. I had been waiting eight weeks for a meal like this one and I lined up poached eggs on muffins, hash browns, tomatoes, mushrooms, a big fruit plate, pastries, a smoothie and orange juice which all tasted amazing after a couple of months of porridge pots. The day after the fight is the strangest feeling because the energy around you takes a massive dive. There are no strict schedules to stick to, the phone is eerily quiet, and the nerves have gone, so I was glad I had a week to relax in the sun with Molly. It was time to focus on her after being absent for a while.

We had managed to keep the pregnancy secret for

six months before we announced it. Molly wore baggy clothes and didn't go to many events. It was such a special time, we wanted it to just be between us for as long as possible so we could enjoy it. So much of our lives plays out in public because of the jobs we do, and we understand that, but we just wanted something for ourselves. We also wanted to be absolutely sure that everything was OK with the baby too.

It was a magical holiday in Dubai, despite Molly being on a bit of an emotional rollercoaster and both of us being very tired. When we were on *Love Island* we were often called Team Sleepy, and we lived up to that nickname on this trip. When we returned to the UK we were refreshed and ready to do the final prep before the baby arrived. I knew it would be a big learning curve, but I was ready to be a father and couldn't wait to meet my daughter. I planned to spend the final couple of months pampering Molly and getting organised for our new life as a family of three. And then I received a phone call.

8

Third Time is a Charm

We were now in charge of this small,
perfect being, her life was our responsibility
and our parental instincts kicked in
immediately. It was the single best, most
magical moment of my life.

The Jake Paul fight was back on the table. Third time lucky. If we couldn't pull it off now it was never going to happen. I truly believe God works in mysterious ways and everything happens for a reason. The fight in Dubai had reignited the tension between us and our teams were back around the table to negotiate, with my lawyer working hard to hash out all the details. Rather than losing interest after two cancelled fights, people had the opposite reaction. It fuelled the expectation and created a frenzy of speculation about when they would see us facing each other in the ring and what the result would be. The purse grew too, so there was even more money at stake now. Had the first fight happened I would have been paid around half of what I was being offered for the third fight, another positive to the whole debacle. The Middle East came in with the best offer and a venue was confirmed in Saudi Arabia.

The date was set for 26 February 2023. Now, this was not good news. My baby was due the month before, which meant I would be training throughout the end of Molly's pregnancy, the birth and then be away for the first weeks of my daughter's life. I think Jake Paul was being crafty because he knew it would disrupt my training and throw me off. We tried to get the date shifted back, but his team said this was the only opportunity. I had pulled out twice before, so I couldn't start dictating terms at this stage. I didn't have a leg to stand on. It was now or never and if it was never, I knew I would be stuck with the ghost of this fight for years to come.

My baby's birth was going to coincide with the point in the fight build-up where I would be away from home for training camp and totally in the zone. Molly and I discussed it. I wasn't going to agree to anything without her complete approval. She and the baby came first, without question, but we also knew what this meant for me career wise, financially and for my mental health. She convinced me to do it. If I backed down at this point, it was game over on so many levels. Instead, I decided to take a different approach from the usual fight countdown and went between training and home rather than disappearing off to a training camp. I am not going to lie, I found it difficult to juggle my two priorities and I constantly felt like I was letting someone down. If I was in the gym, I thought I should be with Molly and if I was with her, I was worried about not being ready for the fight. I was trying to cut myself into a million pieces, but there was nothing to be done about it. I just had to suck it up.

A few weeks before the fight, the point where I am normally in a training camp, I was in the Portland Hospital in London with Molly. The baby wasn't due for another fortnight or so and we were in for a routine check-up when we discovered Molly was already almost two centimetres dilated. This baby wasn't going to wait around and, with advice from the medical team, we decided to go for an induction. We whizzed home for twenty-four hours, packed a bag and then returned to London ready to turn up the next morning for the 7 a.m. appointment at the

Portland. Our last night as just the two of us was spent in a hotel feeling excited, nervous and ready to step into the unknown.

Molly was induced and we were told it would take around six hours to kick start labour, but within ten minutes, she was in a lot of pain, describing it as one long contraction without any let-up. Around midday Molly had an epidural and then the doctor broke her waters. I was fascinated by the whole process and – apart from seeing Molly in pain – I loved it all. By 4 p.m., the doctors were a little unhappy with the baby's heart rate and lack of movement, so they started to talk about a Caesarean section and told me to get into scrubs before going into theatre. I went into the bathroom to get changed but, by the time I came out, they had checked Molly one last time and she had gone from three centimetres to seven centimetres in twenty minutes and then to ten soon after, which meant she was ready to push. No Caesarean was needed and the energy in the room changed instantly as everyone was rushing around getting prepped. Our baby was on her way!

I couldn't believe what I was watching. It was incredible. Molly's legs were up in stirrups, the doctor was using a ventouse suction cup and gently wiggling the baby out in time with the contractions. In those moments, Molly seemed superhuman to me. She was a brave, brilliant warrior and all I could do was hold her hand, stroke her hair and try to be a comfort to her. The baby's head came out, and I was in absolute bits. There was my daughter, crying loudly and in a second, we went from Molly and me to the three of us, a family. I was a snotty mess. I bawled my eyes out, I couldn't hold it together; childbirth was the most beautiful thing I had ever seen. When I first held our baby girl, skin to skin, I looked down at her and I couldn't get my head around the fact she was mine and she had made me a father. We were now in charge of this small, perfect being, her life was our responsibility and our parental instincts kicked in immediately. It was the single best, most magical moment of my life.

We named our baby girl Bambi. This was a name Molly had been sure of for a long time, long before she and I were together. If she had a daughter, she had always wanted to call her Bambi and I really liked the name too, so it was settled. Once we knew we were having a girl, we called her Bambi privately, and we were very used to the name by the time we announced it. There was a bit of a public reaction to it, which really upset Molly at the time, but we could have called her any name and there would have been critics. We love it and that's what matters.

Now Bambi had arrived, safe and healthy, my fight

tears reared up again. Molly was staying in hospital for a few days post-birth and I was sleeping on a camp bed in her room. The hospital was amazing, and we couldn't thank them enough for their professionalism and care, but this was not an environment I could afford to hang around in. I was eating rubbish, slumped on a chair in the room, and I knew my training hours were slipping away. I needed to be at the gym. There was so much riding on this fight; my career was in the balance. After the build-up of two cancelled fights, if I lost to a YouTuber who hadn't been boxing for long, I may as well pack away my boxing gloves.

It was weird to be so ecstatically happy and low at the same time. Every time I tried to enjoy my daughter being born, in the back of my mind there was a voice saying, Yes, but what about the fight? I formed a plan. I spent the nights up with the baby and supporting Molly. In the morning, I dashed to Euston and got the train to Manchester, where I trained and sparred, before heading back to the station and then to the hospital for the evening. I did this for five days. It reminded me of when I was fourteen and the amount of effort it took to travel just for a few hours of training. I grabbed sleep wherever I could whether it was on the train or on the sofa in the hospital room. I don't know how I did it, but I did.

The three of us returned to Cheshire after a week in London and it was so special to bring our daughter into her home. I was there with them both briefly and then I flew to Saudi Arabia. I sacrificed so much in those weeks away, missing the early days of Bambi's life and unable to be there for Molly, and that was a hard thing to accept. I was on FaceTime to Molly every day, and she reassured me they were fine. Her sister, Zoe, stepped in and took my place, and her mum was around so she wasn't on her own and this helped me to relax and focus on the job in hand. Everybody understood I had to go, and Molly was fully behind me. I had no choice and I felt totally supported too because family and friends were checking in on how I was coping – they knew how much I would hate being separated from my girls. The fact was, I wanted to be there, and I wasn't, and it hurts me to this day that I missed so much in the first month, but there we are. It is what it is. I say this a lot, but I find it reassuring when there is nothing to be done about certain situations.

I don't want to be crying 'woe is me', because I am well aware my job also allows me to spend chunks of time at home and I am often able to do stuff in the day with Bambi. I know most other dads get a very brief paternity leave before having to go back to work. I wouldn't change what I do, but there are times when it dictates my life in ways that don't work for my family. This will become more complicated as Bambi gets older and Molly and I hopefully have more children, but for now we make it work because, after all, it is work and I am lucky to have it.

In Saudi Arabia, preparing for the fight, I felt like a different boxer. Now I was a father, and I had the best prize waiting at home for me, so I had already won. It didn't make me any less hungry for the victory though. As Mike Tyson once said, 'a happy fighter is a dangerous fighter'. That is how I felt. Now that Bambi was safely here, I couldn't be any happier, and that also meant I was at my most dangerous. This, coupled with the fact that after two balls-ups I was finally going to face Jake Paul, made me feel invincible. I was more than ready to get in the ring with him and take him down.

I had two weeks to acclimatise to the air, heat and time difference before I fought. The event was outdoors and scheduled for midnight to capture the US and UK audiences, so I had to recalibrate my body clock. Everything was organised for me: training, food, limo transport, massages, press conferences and rest breaks. I was given a three-bedroom suite at one of the best hotels, which must have cost tens of thousands for the fortnight I was there, and this was a certain kind of crazy, but I wasn't complaining. The time leading up to the big night was also focused on my weight, walks with my team and media obligations. The fight was one of the most talked about in recent times so everyone wanted to interview me and visit me in my hotel. I was treated like a king. I knew this was a very different fight from what I was used to, but that only added more flavour to it and boosted my confidence. The press conference was predictably feisty and built the tension for what was to come, and I really enjoyed talking to the media. I had a few verbal scores to settle with Jake Paul before we got into the ring. He had been rude about my missus, had talked about our baby being born before we had announced it and was generally shooting his mouth off.

'It is not about who can talk the best,' I said, 'it's about who can fight the best and he's absolutely rubbish. He's going against someone who wants to take his head clean off with every shot. He's not dealt with that before and it's a big jump. Third time is a charm, and I am in super-fit condition. Ready to go because all it has been for the last two years is "When are you fighting Jake Paul?"' I looked down as I spoke and there was Mike Tyson, in the front row. If my eyes could have popped out on stalks they would have done. When I was a kid and got up at 4 a.m. to go running it was because I had watched him do it and he inspired me. He gave me the motivation to box. I had read his book and seen all his fights; he was my idol. I had met him once, briefly, at one of Tyson's fights, and now there he was, cheering me on and coming to watch me fight. Even if I think about it now, it doesn't sink in. I had dinner with him a few days before the main event, when they got the big names together, and, after my initial shock, we sat chatting comfortably. He was exactly as I had imagined: a humble, down-to-earth guy. What would the fourteen-year-old me have said had he known this is where he would be, only nine years later?! It was another one of those full circles in my life.

At the weigh-in the day before the fight, I was pumped. Not only was I keen to get the job done, but I was also introduced on to the stage by the legendary ring announcer Michael 'let's get ready to rumble' Buffer. It doesn't get any bigger than him in boxing announcing; he has done every big fight worth mentioning and introduced all the greats. I would stay up to watch some of these fights and his voice was an integral part of the experience for me. A few years before I had managed to get a selfie with him at one of Tyson's fights and now there he was, saying my name, Tommy 'TNT' Fury. Unbelievable. I got on the scales and my weight was bang on. Then it was Jake 'The Problem Child' Paul's turn. He weighed in a bit lighter than me. There I was, eight fights with eight wins and there was he, six fights with six wins and neither of us wanted the next to be a loss.

Both sides began to get mouthy, and Jake and I met in the middle of the stage, face to face, our noses touching, and I looked deep into his eyes. I told him he'd had two lucky escapes from this fight, and he should have taken them, he shouldn't have come back for a third time because tomorrow night he was going to lose. I pushed him, we got split up and tensions were as high as they had been at the press conference. I was riled because of some of the stuff he had been saying about me and my family. I think from that moment on he knew he had lost – I saw something in his face. He saw me in the best physical shape, and maybe he realised I hadn't been thrown off guard by becoming a father. I could sense he thought he was beat before we'd even started.

Everything was where it needed to be. I had Dad and my brothers Tyson, Roman, Shane and Hughie there, and Chris and Kyle had flown out to join us. These sorts of big occasions usually happened for Tyson, and I was the one supporting him. Now it was my turn, and he was a great help because he had been through fights bigger than this one, so he could walk me through it all. I had an unbeatable team of professionals and pals around me, and I had never been more grateful for it.

On the morning of the fight, I woke up after ten hours of the best sleep I have had for any of my fights. I felt on top of the world and, after the weigh-in, I could eat again. I think I put on about twelve pounds in twelve hours because I rehydrated and ate masses of carbs. I knew it was going my way. I had a lot riding on this; it was the day I had been waiting for and now it was here I was going to take it with both hands. I said a little prayer before springing out of bed to brush my teeth and do a bit of shadow boxing in the mirror, as you do, well, maybe you don't, perhaps it's just a boxer thing. Or maybe it's just a me thing.

In the kitchen, my food was ready, and I ate my usual pancakes, fruit and oats. I did nothing all day, just lazed around watching a film, conserving my energy. I spoke to Molly, and all was good with her and the baby, which made me feel even better. I would soon be home with them, and I couldn't wait. At around 8 p.m. my security team knocked on the door and said it was time to go. I was fighting in four hours. All I had to do was get myself out of the room, as my kit had already been taken care of. In reception it was like they were waiting for a movie star. There were lights, TV press, my team, fans and limos lined up outside and everyone cheered me to my car.

I put my headphones on and listened to my old boxing theme tune, the Eminem song I had played for my first ever fight. I was so mentally ready; I don't believe I would have lost to anyone that night.

Arriving at the arena felt unreal with the strobe lights, drones and thousands of people turning up. This was so much bigger than the previous two cancelled fights would have been and the production around it was huge: it was an all-singing, all-dancing event and I was there for it. I went to the changing room to chill out for a bit, stretch, chat and relax. I was surrounded by my biggest team to date of security, coaches, a masseuse and a nutritionist, as well as family and friends. Then it was time for me to get my hands wrapped, which is always when I switch into fight mode and shut out everything around me. I think about how I want the fight to go and about my opponent. After warming up on the pads, I felt sharp and I was ready for what was next. My kit was expensive and extra special because it was a Bambi kit, with her name on the waistband of my gold fringed shorts, a picture of a deer and little messages so one day, when she is old enough, she can watch the fight back if she wants to and see how she was my guardian angel for it. I had a long white and gold gown with 'BAMBI' in big lettering on it too.

We were moments away from the fight. I stepped into my trusted routine of rituals. I went into the bathroom, looked at myself in the mirror, made the sign of the cross and asked God to be with me, to look over both fighters. I vowed, if he could grant me the victory, I would give him the glory. I slapped my gloves together and said to my reflection, 'Right, let's do it.' Everyone was waiting anxiously for me, and we got into a big huddle for the team prayer, led by my dad, before there was a knock on the door and the TV crew said we were walking in forty-five seconds. Dad put my hood up and zipped up my jacket. He gave me a nod and I gave him a nod back. This was it.

I was taken into a black, box-like room to wait for my cue, before making my entrance along the walkway to the ring. I stood there alone, bouncing on my toes, and I could hear the crowd going wild and chanting my name. After all this time and so many setbacks, here I was and there was no stopping me.

I walked out to Creedence Clearwater Revival's 'Fortunate Son' and I looked like I meant business with a fresh fade and my hair gelled. I had a nice colour on me, and I'd had my eyebrows done. I was on fire and I felt it too. I know that may sound daft, but personal grooming is important to me, and I think it helps my performance too. The camera was on me as I took it all in: the fans, the arena, the sheer energy that could have lifted me off my feet. My team were following me, Tyson was grinning away a couple of steps behind, and Dad was at my shoulder. This was all for me, and I was ready. I kissed Bambi's name on my jacket and made the sign of the cross as I approached the ring.

Everyone was watching, and I was happy Dad was there because we had gone through so much together. I saluted him, jumped up on the ring apron, kissed my glove and looked up. I could see the iconic footballer Cristiano Ronaldo on his feet in a box and he saluted me. That feeling was surreal. I couldn't address it properly at the time because I was so focused, but I thought about it a lot afterwards. In the moment, I just saluted him back. I knew this was going to be good. Mike Tyson was ringside. All of these men were idols of mine and they were about to watch me, as I had watched them so many times before. But the biggest legends to me – my dad and Tyson – were in the ring, massaging my shoulders and keeping me relaxed.

Jake Paul made me wait for five minutes. I think he was trying to play mind games because the TV cameras were on him, and I could see he was just sat in the changing room. I had worked up a sweat, so I was warm and loose, and maybe he wanted me to go cold. Dad told me not to worry about it, to keep stretching and put a towel over me. Let him take his time, he said. Jake eventually made his walk and got in the ring; I went straight over and told him he was in for it.

We were sent to our corners; introductions were made and I received the biggest cheers that reached the heavens. It appeared that Jake was not very popular. He had never lost before and the boxing community were on my back to take him out because he was not respected as a boxer, he was a YouTuber. I transformed the pressure of that expectation into power.

The Tale of the Tape makes comparisons between the two boxers, and this one showed that we were pretty well matched for a cruiserweight eight-round fight. Jake was twenty-six, three years older than me. I was an inch shorter than him at six foot, and a pound heavier. He was undefeated with six fights, four of them knockouts, and I was undefeated with eight fights and four of them were knockouts too.

We came to the centre of the ring to touch gloves and the referee, Hector Afu, went through the instructions while I stared Jake down. Back in my corner, Dad gave me a hug and a kiss on the head and then he left the ring. It was just me, Jake and the referee in the circle of light, spectators surrounding us under the night sky and the world tuning in from afar. It was being televised globally and even Danny, Molly's sister Zoe's boyfriend, who was in the army, was watching in a bar shack in Kenya.

The bell went for the first round, and it started a bit scrappy. We were getting the measure of each other and settling into the fight. I was hitting him with combinations, putting him on the back foot, and I won the first round. Everything was landing and the crowd was with me. Dad was in my corner with an encouraging pep talk and he was happy with my first round, so I felt good.

In the second round, I came out slipping and sliding. I was enjoying it and I hit him with the first jab, smack in the face, making his long hair fly everywhere. I thought, Have a bit of that! I was up on my toes and in control. In the third round, probably conscious of losing, Jake came out with more energy and got me on the ropes. He was swinging, but unable to land any big shots on me, other than a brush over my eyebrow. I knew I was boxing better, but he had a moment. At the end of the round, Logan Paul, Jake's brother, was interviewed ringside and started shouting about me and my family. His behaviour was considered bad form by the boxing commentators and I doubt it helped Jake's focus.

In round four I was back on top, I felt strong and I was running the show. Jake was looking tired, his face was red and puffy, but he got a shot in. We were halfway through and so far there had been no knock-out, but the general feeling was that I was winning three to one. In round five, Jake got a point taken off for hitting the back of my head and I got a good punch in before the bell. Seconds out, round six and I was feeling comfortable with a right upper cut and a couple of perfect jabs. Jake was holding his own, but it wasn't enough. And then a point got taken off me for holding. Surely not? I felt like he was the one hanging around my neck and he looked pretty beaten. At the end of the round, we were in a clinch and he headbutted me, cutting me above my brow, but it was on the referee's blind side so he didn't get in trouble for it. Maybe it was unintentional, but in that moment it felt like dirty fighting arising from panic because he knew he had two rounds to go and he was losing.

I went back to my corner and sat down on the stool with blood dripping from my eyebrow onto my shorts. The cut was annoying, but I didn't let it slow me down.

'Two rounds to go. Get out there and have a tear up!' Dad said.

I could feel the energy and excitement of the crowd in round seven. It was like they were in the ring with us. I went on the attack and got a few shots in, mid and long, as the seconds ticked down. That was a good round, and other than the cut above my eye, which needed some attention when I went back to the corner, I was in control.

In the final round, I knew I had done enough and just had to stay upright to win. I was in the centre of the ring, and we were exchanging leather when Jake hit me with a jab. I stumbled, but this had nothing to do with the contact he made: the floor was covered in sweat, and it was a genuine slip. As soon as I touched down, I jumped straight back up again because I wasn't hurt, but it was classed as a knockdown and the referee started counting, so I automatically lost, making it a 10/8 round. I was beside myself. I had never been in this predicament before. I turned to Dad.

'That was a slip!' I said, and he nodded in agreement.

'Stay calm, keep focused, move on,' he counselled. I went on the attack, hit Jake with everything and the crowd were roaring. I was on him as if my life depended on it. As soon as the fight ended, I went to the corner, jumped up on the ropes and celebrated because I knew I had won, and the crowd agreed. Jake did the same, but one of us was about to be disappointed and I was pretty sure it wasn't going to be me.

There were so many people milling around in the centre of the ring. In the midst of it were two sweaty, bloody fighters waiting to get the official decision, and I was suddenly overcome with doubt. What if these guys were going to screw me? I don't think I could have coped with them robbing me of this achievement. I shut my eyes in silent prayer. The score cards were being read out. I thought I had won unanimously, but it was now sounding too close for comfort and didn't seem to be going my way: we were even. It didn't reflect the fight I thought I'd had. I had to go to Jake on his own promotion (meaning he was the one who organised and paid for the fight so everything was on his terms) and get the win, which can be tricky and meant the odds would be stacked against me. Sometimes decisions are made that are biased towards the boxer who had set the fight up. I knew I had to win by a clear margin. I thought I had, but I held my breath.

'And the winner, by split decision,' and Michael Buffer paused for what felt like forever, ' . . . Tommmmmmy Fuuuuurrry.' I shouted at the top of my lungs and then I started crying. Everything flashed before my eyes – the broken ribs, being denied access to the States, the online abuse, depression, drinking, hard graft, not being around enough for Molly and leaving my new baby – and, in that moment, it all paid off. The weight had been taken off my shoulders and I felt free and like I could live a happy and content life again. I went over to Jake.

'Fair play, good fight, keep going, you're all right; it's all water under the bridge now,' I said and shook his hand and we hugged. He said it was a great fight and hopefully we could do it again some time and I said it would be a pleasure. There was a lot of respect in the ring at that moment, and I thanked him and his

Taking Bambi back to her roots with her grandad. A special day.

A family holiday in Dubai –
one of our favourite destinations.

Bambi's boogie ball.
Halloween at our house with
all of Bambi's friends.

Bambi at Santa's feet.
She loved Santa so much.

Molly and me sharing a kiss at her mum's wedding.

Tyson and me soaking up the sun in Miami.

Molly and me after my first fight back from *Love Island* – a first-round KO.

Another picture from my first fight back after the love-filled summer.

My dad and me with arms aloft ready to do the job.

James Wiles/Salt and Pepper Media

A photo of me in my American debut. A moment I'll never forget.

A moment at Wembley fighting on Tyson's undercard for the first time!

Dad, Tyson and me walking out for Roman's big fight in Saudi Arabia.

Standing there as the winner with the belt over my shoulder after the fight with Jake Paul!

A kiss on my head from Dad as all the hard work paid off against KSI.

My reaction after beating KSI in my hometown of Manchester.

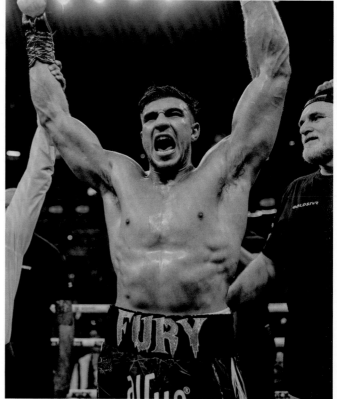

team. I was interviewed wearing the winner's belt and was chock-full of emotion.

'You have every right to shed these tears of victory, glory and joy. You have done something for your family and for your name. You are more than a contender, you are a warrior. Talk to me about the feelings pumping through your heart at this very moment!' The interviewer thrust the microphone at me.

'For the past two and a half years this has consumed my life. Broke a rib, denied access and everyone thought I was running scared. Tonight I made my own legacy. I am Tommy Fury. I want to dedicate this fight to my new baby girl, Bambi, at home, and my missus. I love you and I can't wait to see you. This fight was for you. This belt was for you, Bambi, I love you.' I was in tears now.

'This was no easy fight, it took everything in you, all your heart, grit and soul. How much was inside you when you stood up off this canvas and finished this fight?' the interviewer wanted to know.

'All the way through these two and a half years I had a dream, I had a vision, and nobody believed me. Now I can stand up and everyone can take note. This was my first main event, twenty-three years old and I had the world on me, I had pressure on my shoulders, and I came through.' More cheers from the arena and clapping from my brothers. Dad's grin couldn't get any bigger. The interviewer kept going.

'I know your goal is to be a world champion, but this belt you are holding now must be awfully sweet.'

'This to me is a world-champion fight. I have trained so hard for this, it is my destiny, my fate. I want to thank Saudi Arabia for having me. I love you all and thank you all for turning out. We did it!'

'Now we know that Jake Paul has a rematch clause; he may want to do this again and if so, will we see you back here for another war of this magnitude?' I already knew the answer to this.

'One hundred per cent. It's my first main event and I am only going to go stronger and bigger and better. There are a lot of nerves coming into here and I can override that. If he wants a rematch, then bring it on!' The interviewer nodded and wrapped up our chat: 'For showing up and giving us all that you had, congratulations on an incredible win.'

No sooner had I given that interview I was asked by BT Sport how I was feeling.

'Tears of joy. Jake was a true warrior and a better man than I thought, but at the end of the day this has consumed my life; nobody thought I could do it and everyone thought I was running scared.'

This interviewer asked me about the round eight knockdown and whether it had shocked me.

'I will be honest and there are no excuses coming from me, that was not a knockdown, it was a slip, genuinely. I got up, I wasn't hurt, and I came right back into it.' And did I rate him as a boxer, was he tougher than I thought?

'One hundred per cent. He gave some good shots and at the end of the day he is far better than I thought he was.' So what did I want out of this, the interviewer asked.

'Right now, I want to see my missus and my baby girl and spend some time at home.'

Then Jake Paul was interviewed.

'All respect to Tommy, he won. Don't judge me by my wins, judge me by my losses. I'll come back and I think we deserve that rematch. It was a great fight, a close fight and I don't know if I agree with the judges, but it is what it is, this is boxing.' Yep, Jake, it is what it is.

Back in the packed changing room, Tyson started a chant of 'There's only one Tommy Fury!' and everyone joined in. I had a beautiful baby girl and I had won my biggest fight: this was the best time of my life.

After half an hour, I went to the medical room to get my eye stitched up as I had been holding it until then. I ran into Jake Paul who was in there to get checked over. We had a chat because there were no cameras there, and we got a photo together. He said he hoped to run the fight back one day and I said I would love to do it again. We shook hands and he went his way and I went mine with a new shared respect for each other. Business concluded. We knew how to sell a show and we made history as the most viewed fight of that year and one of the most viewed ever. Jake and I did that. I congratulated him too because it takes two to tango and he was a great dance partner.

I called Molly. She had not been able to watch because she was too nervous, so had been upstairs in our bed, breastfeeding Bambi in the dark, without the TV on or her phone next to her. Zoe was there and a couple of friends had come over, so they were downstairs watching the fight. When I won, she heard joyful screaming from downstairs, Zoe raced up to tell her the good news and they jumped around on the bed.

There is an alcohol ban in Saudi, which meant there was no chance of a post-fight blow-out. Instead, everyone came back to my hotel suite, and we ordered kebabs and burgers. On the morning of the fight, I had gone out to the Cheesecake Factory and bought a slice of every single cheesecake they made. I spent a small fortune because it was one of the forbidden foods I had been fixated on throughout camp. I stocked up and must have brought back at least forty wedges of cheesecake. I had even moved all the healthy stuff out of the fridge to make room and I neatly stacked the cheesecakes in the order I wanted to eat them. I was surrounded by family and mates, we ate well and had great laughs and then I went to bed. I had won the fight in front of almost everyone I cared about, with a few of my idols chucked in for good measure. Those memories will last for ever.

Coming home to be a family man was the real win. I couldn't wait to change nappies and do all the things I had missed out on. I wanted the simple pleasures of getting into bed with Molly, with Bambi sleeping next to us, and being the one to get up in the middle of the night when she cried. The first thing we did when I got back was to go out to the local cafe for a burger and chips like we often did, but now with the baby in the pram next to us. Sat there with a plaster over my eye – a reminder of the fight – and my beautiful Molly opposite me, I thought, This is as good as life gets.

Of course, the reality of looking after a tiny baby is not all sunshine and rainbows (to quote *Rocky*) and those early months were harder than I ever imagined they would be. As wonderful as it is, it is also exhausting with interrupted nights, crying for reasons we were still trying to understand and the sheer terror and responsibility of keeping this small being alive. I was head over heels in love with my baby girl and also poleaxed by the changes her arrival made to our lives. Molly is an amazing mum, and she took to it brilliantly, but that doesn't mean there weren't difficult days to navigate, and emotions often ran high. As soon as Bambi began smiling at us, we reached a new level of bonding and we really turned a corner when she was around six months old and her little personality began to shine out of her.

Following the Jake Paul fight, it was like *Love Island* all over again: everyone wanted a piece of me, a short tour of public appearances was organised and a couple of restaurants even refused to charge me when I went for dinner. It was lovely to be recognised for all the right reasons and I got approached to take part in several high-profile events including an invitation to join Soccer Aid.

I am not a footballer. I am pretty terrible at the game, and I couldn't even make the local church team as a kid, so when Soccer Aid got in touch, I really wasn't sure about doing it. What convinced me was the charity aspect; I was keen to work with UNICEF, so I put my ineptitude to one side and thought I could get away with running up and down the pitch, if I didn't have to kick the ball too often. At least I had the stamina for it, if not the goal-scoring abilities. I wasn't sure what I had let myself in for, but it turned out to be one of the most fun experiences of my life. We all met at Champneys spa hotel in Tring and the room was packed with famous people: actors, singers, comedians, athletes and ex-professional footballers. I looked around and I thought, I should not be here. I was not on their level, everyone there was high profile and the sportspeople were at Olympic-standard levels. I was definitely not worthy, but I was thrilled to be among them all.

In the middle of the afternoon on the first day everyone had a beer, and the place became a party. It was a brilliant icebreaker and completely private because nobody else was staying in the hotel. We had the place to ourselves so we could relax and get to know each other. Every morning we trained, and the afternoons were ours and we all met in the evening for drinks, dinner and even karaoke. One night, at the bar, I had a long chat with Sir Mo Farah about swapping roles and him getting in the boxing ring while I ran long distance. That was certainly not a conversation I ever thought I would be having.

Usain Bolt was one of the captains and he had asked for me on his team, which was incredible. So too was walking out at Old Trafford after going as a child with my grandad back when Ronaldo was playing there. I was in the tunnel and the noise was deafening as we came out into a packed stadium and lined up on the pitch. Going from being high up in the stands to right in the centre of the action felt like another full-circle moment. I looked around me and I was surrounded by famous people; it was like being in a surreal dream where I found myself about to play football with Danny Dyer, Jill Scott, Paddy McGuinness, Lee Mack and Patrice Evra, and any minute now I was going to wake up. When Usain scored a goal, I ran up to him and we high-fived and embraced. I had grown up watching him at the Olympics and then there I was, in his football team, being watched by seventy thousand people in the stands and more than four million viewers at home. It was a sensational experience from start to finish and we raised over fourteen million pounds, so I hope it is something I can be part of for many years to come.

I was also asked to take part in a brand campaign for the fashion label Diesel; I'm a fan of the brand anyway, but they took me on a trip to Milan! I am not a natural model – it's not something I have done a lot – but I was keen to pursue it and it was good to stretch myself. About a week before the shoot, I did not like the way I looked, but with a zero-carb diet I managed to get myself into the sort of shape I was happy with, and I was pleased with the way the photos turned out. I worked with an excellent team, and I got to spend a couple of days in a fabulous Italian city full of amazing restaurants. I couldn't eat before the shoot, but as soon as it was over, I set myself a challenge to consume ten thousand calories, which I know sounds mad, but after burgers, milkshakes, fries, pasta, crêpes, chocolate and gelato, I did it.

This was partly to help build my YouTube channel, which is relatively sparse as far as content goes as I haven't had the focus to invest in it properly. When I have spare time, I want to do something to get my endorphins going, not get stuck down a social media rabbit hole. That said, I am keen to do more on my own channel and I really like vlogging about exercise, travel and food so I plan to do more of it. I also enjoy making these videos with my friend, the former world's strongest man Eddie Hall. He has a similar background to me. He's a cracking fella, a normal guy from Stoke, who has done really well; it's great to hang out with him and his family at his house or in the gym.

We set each other challenges like who can punch the hardest on a punchbag machine (spoiler alert, Eddie beat me by a whisker), who can lift the most, and can we eat twenty-five burger patties (of course we can). We get lots of feedback about our on-screen chemistry and I would love to think we can do more as a double act in the future.

Many of these opportunities would not have been possible if I had stayed within a traditional boxer role and stuck to the well-trodden career path. The sport has changed so much in the last ten years, and I have been part of that shift, straddling two worlds: that of traditional boxers and that of influencers. I had some really interesting conversations after the Jake Paul fight, both within and beyond the boxing community. People who had never been interested in the sport before had watched the fight because of the huge amount of hype around it, and some die-hard fans – the purists who want proper boxers – were furious with this development. I can see both sides because I have been on both sides.

Professional boxing is a serious and skilled job. That's not to say that those YouTubers who cross over into the sport don't take it seriously or are lacking in talent, it's just that a social-media-led approach turns the whole thing into more of a spectacle. It is the Las Vegas of boxing. There is so much more money on the line, the events sell out and there are millions of pay-per-view spectators. It brings with it a brand-new audience, a fan base that crosses all age ranges, demographics and cultures, which is never a bad thing. This is where sport meets showbusiness and I think there is a place for it.

Proper boxers will get upset about YouTubers because they have worked all their lives to get into the ring, they have trained hard, come through the amateurs, turned professional and now they are getting on with the job. I understand because I am one of them, which also entitles me to share my opinion on this phenomenon. Most fighters are not even earning two per cent of the money the YouTubers are getting, but that is the way boxing has changed (like so many other professions). It's not just about how well you can fight, it's about how many bums you can put on seats, and if you can fill an arena, promoters will get you where you want to go. It's called prize fighting after all, and stepping into the ring is all about fighting for the prize.

So, when I make the decision between fighting Adam Jones from Norfolk (a fictitious boxer I have just made up for the purposes of making this point) for some loose change or Jake Paul for life-changing money, guess what I am going to pick? Why wouldn't I? Wouldn't you? I am risking my life whoever I face, and when the stakes are that high you want the reward to match it. This matters even more now I have a family to support. You never know how long you have in this game, and you don't know when your time is up. While I can't imagine retiring, it will happen, and I have to be pragmatic. The aim of boxing is to get in, make as much money as you can and then get out, bearing in mind the annoying caveat to this which is how addictive the sport is. Still, that's the basic formula for a boxing career. Floyd Mayweather Jr was asked a question in a press conference following his fight with Logan Paul in 2021 about the criticism he came in for when choosing to fight a YouTuber. He gave one of the best answers of all time:

They say 'It's not all about the money' ... well, your kids can't eat legacy. Patches on my trunk, that's $30 million alone. So who's really the smartest one in the sport of boxing? If you guys don't wanna see me do no exhibitions, don't come. Don't watch. When it comes to legalised bank robbing, I'm the best. I don't care if y'all write good stories, I don't care if y'all write bad stories. At the end of the day, I will always have the last laugh.

For me, it's about the sport and it's about being the best, but it's also about not wasting the hours, days, weeks, months and years of training on making very little money. At this stage in my life, my attitude has changed, from wanting to buy nice things for myself to focusing on Bambi and making sure she will always be OK. I want her to have a lovely house, food in the fridge and a safe, secure environment to grow up in.

There is a lot of jealousy and hate around the YouTuber fights, but let's be clear, whatever your background or reasons for being there, you are still in the ring, swapping leather, risking your health and reputation. You have to be at a certain level to cope with this. Take Jake Paul as an example. He may be a rival of mine, but I can respect his work ethic and commitment to the sport. I also applaud some of the issues he has tackled in the boxing world, championing overlooked female boxers like the Puerto Rican professional Amanda Serrano, pushing for unionisation and calling for fair pay. Jake isn't just coming in and taking the money; he is using his voice for the greater good.

All of that said, there are fights I don't agree with, and the combination of Jake Paul and Mike Tyson makes me uncomfortable, I don't think it should be allowed. My dad has been calling Mike out for years, and that is a better match. I think there are some fights that should stay in the imagination for fear that they could undermine something both boxers have worked hard to build. Mike is sixty, he is a living legend, so God forbid anything goes wrong. Although I feel like the boxers of his generation and before were better men, as the years have passed, the fighter's attitude and ability have changed along with the sport. Perhaps we are softer now, faced with eight or twelve rounds rather than fifteen. It's all about health and safety. I think the boxers of yesteryear could wipe the floor with the lot of us.

As for me and Jake Paul, now the dust has settled, would I fight him again? You betcha I would! I only mention him when he mentions me, but he seems to do that all the time, so maybe he isn't over me. We will meet again in the ring; it is only a matter of time. I respect him and I am more than ready for him. Next time, I will be victorious again, except this time around it will be a knockout. You have been warned, Jake!

9

The Vow

I kissed Molly, handed her Bambi and gave a little speech before going down on one knee and opening the ring box. I asked her if she would make me the proudest man on earth.

Molly and I had been together for almost four years and for much of that time, we were constantly asked when we would get married. Although I knew she was the person I wanted to spend the rest of my life with, I didn't want to jump into a proposal. We had talked about it and even gone to look at engagement rings together, so I knew what she liked, but it never felt like the perfect time to ask her. We were both so busy and there was always something going on, whether it was Molly's career or mine, and then Bambi's arrival; it never felt like either of us was in the right headspace.

After the Jake Paul fight, when I had been back home for a couple of weeks, I had this overwhelming sense of peace and happiness. I knew this was the year to make it official with Molly, and I decided to propose in the summer and create a magical moment to remember. Surprising Molly is virtually impossible, so I'd set myself a hard task – and I wanted Bambi to be there too.

I spent a couple of months thinking about the best way to do it, and then I started planning it properly. I didn't want to take her to a local restaurant and go down on one knee before the pudding came out (not that there is anything wrong with that); I wanted to make her feel like a movie star. If I took Molly on holiday, she would have an inkling because whenever we went away there was speculation about whether this was the time. I knew it would go through her mind and I would blow it by making it too obvious. She is incredibly perceptive, and I was bound to make a blunder, so I had to use everything at my disposal to pull this off.

Molly goes to events all around the world, so I came up with the idea to invite her to one of the most exclusive, luxury parties full of A-listers in the hope that she would say yes. I chose Net-a-Porter because they throw actual events so I thought that would be more believable – although obviously the event didn't exist on the date we were supposedly going. Imagine the sort of prank that Ant and Dec do on *Saturday Night Takeaway* that results in the best outcome for the unwitting target. That was what I had in my mind. Like them, it would take more than me to make it happen; I would need to pull in a team of helpers.

I printed an invitation and told Molly's manager, Fran, what I was doing. She was immediately on board. She contacted Molly to say she and I had been invited to this prestigious event in Ibiza and she really sold it to her, making it sound amazing. Fran also said Molly had been given an allowance to buy a dress for the evening from the Net-a-Porter website, which I was secretly funding because poor Net-a-Porter obviously knew nothing about this. The outfit would be the one she would think she was wearing for the party when in fact, it was for my proposal.

Behind the scenes, there was a lot of work to do including booking hotels, working out travel plans and trying to keep everything hush hush for a couple of months, which is no mean feat when you live with Molly, I can tell you. I had to keep my phone close to me at all times, which began to arouse suspicion.

She has always jumped on my phone to play music or look at photographs on my camera roll, but I was concerned she would see a message relating to Mission Proposal and I couldn't risk a single slip-up.

The weekend before we were due to go, we were putting Bambi to bed, and I casually asked Molly if she was looking forward to the event and she said she didn't think she would go. Not go?! NOT GO?! Dear God, after all the time, preparation, secrecy and, quite frankly, cost involved I nearly passed out. I tried to remain calm. She said she had thought about it, and she just wanted to be at home with Bambi and hated leaving her. In my mind there were bombs going off. Months of planning had gone into this, and I was so close to making it happen, I couldn't let her pull out. Between me, her manager and her hair and make-up team, who she thought Net-a-Porter had booked to come with us (when in fact it was me), we persuaded her to go.

'You might as well,' we all told her, repeating each other, 'it's all laid on, enjoy yourself and get a bit of sun. You will never know who you might meet, and you will have a great time.' It took about ten of us separately to say the same thing, but eventually we convinced her. The stress of it nearly made me blurt everything out on more than one occasion, but I managed to keep my cool.

We flew out of Manchester and once we were on the plane, I could tick off the first stage of the mission. Molly was happy and looking forward to the event after we had all convinced her she would have fun. When we checked into the hotel, there was a letter from Net-a-Porter (yep, me) in our room, welcoming us to Ibiza and saying how much they were looking forward to hosting us. If I didn't already know, I would have genuinely thought we were there for work, and Molly was completely convinced by it. Phew! Molly's team arrived and started to get her ready, chatting about what she could expect from the evening. They played their part brilliantly. Molly had chosen her outfit, a white shoulderless jumpsuit, which couldn't have been better if she had known what it was actually for. She looked absolutely stunning.

Now, this is a little complicated, so bear with me. Jake, my manager, was in Marbella at the time and he had the engagement ring. I'd had it made, and it was being kept at a jewellery shop in London for safety, so he'd picked it up and hung on to it for me. The poor man must have almost buckled under the weight of responsibility, but he took it in his stride as he does everything. He happened to be in Marbella when we arrived in Ibiza, so I had to fly him over with the ring and he turned up, looking like he was just popping in to check on everything before the event. He was chatting to Molly with the ring in his pocket and she had absolutely no idea.

I paid for everyone to come over. I don't know who I thought I was. I threw some money around and went a bit mad, behaving like I was Jeff Bezos or Bill Gates. I knew this was what it was going to take. Everyone went along with it and did so well, it was like being surrounded by paid actors, which is what it took to surprise Molly. Anything less and she would have guessed. She would have pretended that she didn't know, just to go along with it and not ruin it for me, and I didn't want to risk that. She is always one step ahead, so I had to work doubly hard to keep her in the dark, and by God, I was just about managing to do it.

Once we were ready, we took some photos as we would before any event and the car came to pick us up and take us to the Hacienda Hotel. Even the driver was in on it and asked if we were looking forward to the Net-a-Porter party. He said he had heard it was amazing. Give the man an Oscar! In the car, Molly asked if she could have a look at the pictures we had taken of us on my phone. I hadn't thought this through; I was potentially about to be scuppered at the last moment. I immediately panicked because if she went onto my camera roll, she would see photos I had just been sent of the setting of our proposal, or a message might pop up that would give the game away. I was so close; I couldn't let that happen. I made a lame excuse about being in the middle of a texting debate with my dad about a fight contract. It caused a massive argument because by this point, she thought I was having an affair. She had always used my phone and now I was refusing to hand it over, so she thought I might be messaging another girl. I was fuming. I couldn't believe she would think that, but I also had to remind myself that I was acting shifty, so it was fair enough.

Ten minutes before I was due to propose, I almost called the whole plan off because we were in the middle of this blazing row. God knows what the poor driver thought. At this point the car turned into the 'event' at the Hacienda. I had hired the cliff at the back of the hotel for the proposal. I didn't even know you could rent a cliff, but there you are, it turns out you can and so I did because that was the sort of mad decision-making that I had got myself into for the proposal. It sounds unbelievable, I know. We arrived mid argument and I just jumped out of the car and shut the door so Molly couldn't follow me. I had to sprint to the scene and get myself into position, but I can see how ridiculous this must have looked.

As I legged it, Molly was almost in tears, thinking I was in a huff and had abandoned her. This was not ideal, but I couldn't do anything about it in that moment or I'd risk blowing the surprise. As planned, the woman from the hotel came to the car and handed Molly a letter which said there was no event, and the hotel would show her where to go. She was totally nonplussed by this point.

My brother Roman had flown over with Bambi and they were there waiting for me, so I took her from him and made my way to the spot, surrounded by the most amazing flower arrangements, looking out across the ocean. I had also booked the singer RuthAnne to perform her song 'The Vow', which was one of Molly's favourites. It had been played in the *Love Island* final, and Molly fell in love with it and wanted to play it at our engagement, whenever that was going to be, as it meant so much to us. I don't think she ever expected RuthAnne to actually be there singing it, but she was in position, waiting to be cued and I had the ring in my pocket and Bambi in my arms. Molly come round the corner as RuthAnne began to sing and she saw her and then she saw us, the flowers and the ocean view. She started to cry, tears of joy I hoped, and I felt very emotional too, but I had to keep it together for a little longer. I kissed Molly, handed her Bambi and gave a little speech before going down on one knee and opening the ring box. I asked her if she would make me the proudest man on earth.

'Will you marry me?'

She said yes. At least it sounded like yes, but it was hard to make out as she was uncontrollably crying by this point. I hoped that meant she loved the surprise and hadn't guessed what was going on. She said she had absolutely no idea, although she knew it was likely I would do something like this, but even in the middle of it all, as it was happening right in front of her eyes, she hadn't cottoned on. We hugged and the three of us stood looking at the breathtaking view. It had gone better than I could have imagined – even the argument in the car added to the drama of occasion.

Roman took Bambi back to our hotel and Molly and I went out for dinner where I had booked a treehouse dining space for a four-course meal and celebratory champagne. We took it all in – the amazing food, views and being newly engaged – then called our family to tell them. I was so happy it had worked out. I had wanted it to be really special, to wow her and sweep her off her feet, and I think I did that. We were having such a great year and I wanted it to continue. I planned the engagement date for 23 July to tie in with Bambi's birth on 23 January because that is the sort of old romantic I am and dates are important to me.

The team who had helped me pull it off went home and Molly and I had a few days together with Bambi. I needed a long lie down on a nice sun lounger after all the planning and stress of it all! People in the hotel came up to congratulate us and when we got home there were balloons and flowers from family and friends. It was a true celebration of our relationship and commitment to each other.

There was one other secret I had kept from Molly. I had asked her father for her hand in marriage a couple of weeks previously. One day, just before Bambi's bedtime routine, I told her that Tyson had called to say he had someone available to spar with me and I needed to go to Morecambe for a training session. This wasn't unusual, so Molly didn't think anything of it. I kissed them both goodbye and said I would call when I was on the way back. Little did she know that in my gym bag, instead of my boxing gloves, were my best clothes.

I drove to the Shell garage at the bottom of the road, went into the toilet, changed into my suit and did my hair. I had gone in looking like a troll in smelly gym gear and I came out looking like John Travolta in *Saturday Night Fever*. I drove to Chester, where Molly's dad lives, and he had booked a nice restaurant. I had messaged him a few days before to invite him out for dinner and would he mind not mentioning anything to Molly, so he knew what was coming. It was great to see him, and he handled it so well because it was pretty nerve-wracking for me. I had obviously never done it before and neither had my friends, so I didn't have anyone to ask for advice. I just had to wing it.

We talked for the first hour about everything, including training, fights, what was coming up and how Bambi was, then we looked at each other. He said he knew why I was there, and he asked me how I was going to propose and what it was I loved about his daughter. It was a magic conversation and I felt very relaxed. He gave me his blessing. On the way home, I stopped at the garage to change back into my gym gear, messed my hair up, splashed water on myself for a little bit of sweat and came back through the door at 10 p.m. Molly was none the wiser.

I was determined to show Molly how much she meant to me, and I think I did that.

A week after Molly and I announced our engagement, there was a second announcement. My next fight would be against KSI.

Jake Paul's number-one rival was KSI and they were meant to fight each other before Jake and I fought. As I had beaten Jake, it put me in line to fight KSI. Apart from a rematch, which Jake didn't want at the time, KSI was the next option and it made financial sense too. The Jake Paul fight was my last under Frank Warren's banner before I got my own licence and became self-managed, so for the KSI fight, I went under his promotional company, Misfits. As well as all the practical points, there was another reason why I wanted to get in the ring. There was genuine bad blood between me and KSI.

When I came out of *Love Island* I was giving an interview and someone asked if I would fight KSI; I said yes I would, no problem. He had been going on about it and saying that I needed the fight way more than he did. A few short years later, there he was, asking me for a fight because I had beaten Jake Paul. I hadn't warmed to his persona, nor did I like the sound of some of his behaviour – it didn't sit right with me – so I was ready to face him in the ring.

It was set up for me to fight KSI on 14 October at Manchester Arena, in my hometown. My tenth fight was to be at the same venue as my first professional bout, which was a nice link. It sold out within a few days and was on course to break records on pay-per-view: another big fight which required the same mindset and piled on the usual pressure. The week after Ibiza, before my training camp began on 7 August, I did a bit of running and cleaned up my diet in readiness for what was to come.

With each fight, I have learned more about myself as a person, my physical strength, my mental capacity, and also how much I love food! It's one of my biggest joys in life and it means that I tend to pile on the pounds between training camps and then have to lose it again before a big fight. I don't want to keep yoyoing drastically and I have been focusing more on these in-between times. I've spent most of my life ignoring the value of a sensible, structured diet and taking very little notice of nutrition, so the last couple of years have been a big learning curve. But I have now found a plan that works for me, considering the amount of exercise I do outside of training camps.

This time around, we had done a deal for me to set up my training camp at Mottram Hall spa in Cheshire. They built me a gym on the complex and my team and I stayed there for the duration of the training timetable. I had to push all the excitement of the engagement and the comfort of home behind me as I now had another task to focus on.

The camp was for ten weeks, the longest I had done to date, and I needed to work hard because I hadn't trained seriously since February. I was doing shuttle runs and I could feel it; I was not in the best shape and felt goose tired (something my dad said a lot when I was little which has become my way of describing how particularly knackered I can feel after training). I had to dig deeper than I ever had before, to reach another level and crack on. The first two weeks were really tough because I was overweight, my timing was off and everything was difficult, but I had no idea then that this would be the easiest part of the countdown.

At the beginning of the third week, things went from bad to worse when I started sparring.

In 2019, during my first fight back after *Love Island*, I had sustained a knuckle injury and torn the ligaments in my hand. It was pretty nasty, and I needed an operation, but I put it off after the fight because I didn't want to take the time out for a long recuperation. With each fight it was getting progressively worse. I did everything I could to protect my knuckle during training, even using yellow household sponges under my wraps to soften the impact. They became the most unlikely talisman and made me feel safer. There is always talk of new products to use and different ways to do things, but if it works for you, don't change it. I want practical, not flash and fancy.

During the second round of sparring, I hit this guy with a flush shot, connected properly, and then I felt a shock, like a bolt of electricity, go all the way up my arm to my neck. I was in so much pain and I had to finish the rest of the session one-handed. By the end my hand had gone numb, and when I took my glove off it had swollen up like a balloon. I had never seen it like that before. My knuckle was badly inflamed and had turned a strange shade of purple. The spar session had been in the evening, so I was in the hospital at midnight waiting to be seen. The X-ray showed everything – torn ligaments and bone damage. It was really serious, and the borrowed time I had been on had run out.

I went back to Mottram and sat down with Dad and my manager because we had a decision to make. Nobody outside of my team knew this had happened. It was either postpone the fight and have the operation or push on through and book the op in afterwards. The first plan would have taken me out of the sport for months, and I didn't want that after coming off a good win against Jake Paul. I knew only too well the hassle that would come with cancelling the event and I couldn't face it, nor did I want to lose out on the money. I wanted to continue and that was final.

Dad was worried and questioned my reasons for going ahead. He reacted both as a father and as my coach. He tried to persuade me to think again, saying my opponent wouldn't have this problem and was I sure I didn't want to put the fight off. I was sure. I had already had to deal with two cancellations with Jake Paul, the event was sold out and it was my home crowd so I couldn't back out. And yet again I was billed as the professional boxer who was pitted against the YouTuber and I couldn't let my sport down either. As I have said before, YouTubers aren't expected to win, they are there for the payday, transferring their following into ticket-purchasing arena audiences and home viewers as a money-making business. Former world champions and sports analysts were currently discussing how I had to save boxing in the face of this new mistrusted trend.

I decided I would get through camp by using my left hand for the next seven weeks and not use my right hand until the week of the fight. I would have to spar one-handed. I rang the doctor who had originally treated my injury and had given me a cortisone injection before my Jake Paul fight because my hand was playing up then too. I asked him if I could get through camp with my one hand and if he would be OK to give me the injection in fight week and whenever I needed it. He was happy to do that. And what do us Fury lads say? You guessed it, 'there's no use crying over spilt milk', 'let's get on with the job' and 'what's for you won't pass you by'! I had put as much as I could in place, and I had to trust that it would work out. From the third week onwards, I only used my left hand.

Most training days in camp looked the same: it was like being in a really fancy prison where I would go between my bedroom, the gym and the spa. I got up early and straight into an ice bath. It's all about doing stuff you don't want to do, and when you first open your eyes, and you are cosy in bed, you do not want to get into freezing water. That said, it is the quickest way to wake up and get those endorphins racing around my body. We would then head out for a six-mile run, driving to a spot where we could incorporate some hills, and I sneaked in a morning FaceTime with Molly and Bambi because they were usually up by then. Once back, I stretched out, had a shower and then sat down to the breakfast my nutritionist had organised for me, so it was always a surprise. One of my favourites was pancakes with fruit, two boiled eggs and black coffee. I had a mid-morning nap break followed by lunch – usually something like salmon, rice and vegetables – then into the pool for an intense forty-five-minute workout, where I would front crawl competing against Roman while Dad shouted instructions. In the evening there might be a sparring session or training on the bags. Then bed. Eat, sleep, train, repeat.

This time the camp was physically and mentally tough because I couldn't get the best out of myself; I was using one hand against people who had two. In addition, any movement hurt my right hand and at night it throbbed continually, so it interrupted my sleep. I loved being at Mottram Hall, but because of my injury, it was the worst camp I have endured.

A few weeks before the fight we had the first press conference interview in London, which also included Logan Paul and Dillon Danis, the other boxers fighting on the night. It was chaos, with all of us talking over each other, then KSI and I jumped up and were held apart by security. Dad was wound up by the lack of proper boxing talk as Logan and Dillon resorted to slagging off each other's love lives and Logan brought out a cake of a knocked-out Dillon. There was a moment of intensity and then all hell broke loose. Dad kicked the tables off the stage and there was a lot of scuffling as security stepped in. Logan picked up the head from the Dillon cake and threw it at him, microphones and bottles were chucked, and the place erupted again. Someone shouted out, 'That's a wrap!' and the conference was over. We were swiftly herded out.

On fight week I had the cortisone injection, with three needles, one either side of the knuckle and one in the knuckle itself. My hand went numb and throughout the week I got it topped up so I could throw the punches, although as soon as the injection wore off it was even more painful because I had been using it. I regularly questioned my decision to forge ahead, but it was too late now. There was no going back.

The second press conference was the Wednesday before the Saturday fight, at the Crowne Plaza hotel in Manchester. I arrived to crowds of people shouting my name as I was ushered inside, flanked by security. We were in a room, waiting for the event to start, when I glanced out of the window: there was the bus stop I used to wait at on my way to the gym. As a young teenager, I would stare at the hotel when I was bored and cold, waiting for the bus, and now, less than ten years later, I was looking out at it from the hotel, ready for one of the biggest fights of my career so far. Another full-circle moment.

Parked in the bus bay were two double-deckers promoting the fight: one had my face on it, the other KSI's. In that moment it really hit me. It may seem far-fetched, but this is my story, it's the truth, as it happened. It really took me back to a time before the fans, the press and the face on the bus. This was where I spent hours waiting when I was trying to make a name for myself and build a positive future. Now I was headlining one of the biggest fights of the year. I couldn't put it into words; it was another pinch-me moment, and I had an out-of-body experience, like I was watching the film of my life. The bus stop and the shops hadn't changed but my life had, although I haven't as a person. I am still the same guy who waited at that bus stop in all weathers, trying to do the best he can and better himself.

Everyone was prepared at this press conference after the behaviour at the last one. I was the first out. I said my fists would do the talking on Saturday night and I was there to make a statement. KSI was going to lose.

'Is he a better boxer than me? No. Is he faster than

me? No. Can he hit harder than me? No.' KSI came out in a lime green suit and dark glasses and was straight on the attack, insulting my dad following the upset at the previous meeting, so they immediately got into an argument. Someone threw a plastic bottle and Dad was blamed even though it wasn't him. The abuse was flying between us and building up the tension for the fight.

'All the talking is done,' I said. 'Forty-eight hours and it's over for you, mate.'

There was a steel cage on stage, and we were both asked to get in it for the face off because they didn't trust us after the last time. I stripped off my T-shirt to show KSI what he was up against, and he seemed reluctant to do the same, but he did, and we goaded each other. He was smaller than me and I knew I could take him. We had an argument about sparring partners: he was obsessed with who had been in my training gym, as if that would prove anything. Enough of this, I thought.

'You're in my house now,' I warned him, 'this is my hometown.'

Someone told my dad to get in the cage too and he threw a few punches at the Perspex screen which separated us from KSI. Boxing is a sport which has been around for thousands of years, but it is also the entertainment business, and the build-up adds to it and encourages viewers. That said, the taunts I made and the insults I threw were not just for the cameras.

Fight day arrived. I was in Mottram Hall doing what I always did, resting during the day, eating as usual and Molly came to see me. At around 4 p.m. I had the cortisone injections in my knuckle, ready for the 11 p.m. fight, and then it was time to go to the arena. I was travelling in a big minibus with my team, my headphones were on, and I tried not to think about my hand. I had never gone into a fight in this much pain. It was playing on my mind: was I about to make a dick of myself after stubbornly refusing to cancel the fight? It was too late to doubt my decision now; I had to block out any negative thoughts and get on with it.

There was an incredible vibe in the arena. It was packed to the rafters and the crowd were buzzing with adrenalin. It was a bigger audience than the Jake Paul fight and I could feel the energy in the place; it lifted me up and reminded me of the big fights I'd watched growing up. In the changing room, I had everyone around me. There was a TV on, and it was showing what was happening live in the arena. Only five years earlier I'd been a nervous boy about to make my professional debut in front of a much smaller crowd, and now I was headlining the main event in the same arena: there has been so much serendipity in this career of mine so far.

I followed my usual routine and got my hands wrapped, warmed up, hit the pads, gave myself a stern talking to in the toilet mirror and then the TV crew knocked on the door with a two-minute warning. I was in an orange and black kit because it was October, and I wanted it to pay tribute to Halloween, my favourite time of year. Molly designed the outfit to reflect this, and I had the best shorts, covered in sparkling crystals. I was so shiny you could have seen me from the moon. I put my robe on with 'FURY' emblazoned over the front, my hood went up, Dad led the team prayer, then I made the sign of the cross and walked out, in the exact same direction the nineteen-year-old me had.

As I was in my hometown and it was Halloween, I employed six dancers, for the first time ever, to do the ring walk with me. My old friend Michael Buffer was there to introduce us, the crowd went wild and then the lights cut out. I got the chills as I was waiting on the stairs to the main stage. It was like walking into a starry night because the arena was dark, lit only by around twenty thousand iPhones. Michael Jackson's 'Thriller' started playing, and I was there with my zombie dancers. I put my hood down, stopped for a minute and took it in. It surpassed all my previous experiences. I did a little dance, blew a few kisses and I thought, regardless of the hand injury, I am not losing tonight.

I went through my usual routine of bouncing off the ropes and saluting the crowd. I could see my family and friends on the first row – my brothers were jumping around but Molly had her head down, unable to watch. KSI was introduced and as he came out, the crowd booed him. We touched gloves and went to our corners. I shared the same moment with my dad as always, he left the ring and then we were down to business. Nobody else existed other than my opponent, opposite me in the pool of light.

If there was ever anyone who didn't want to fight, it was him. I went to the middle expecting to begin and he came out doing star jumps and it threw me because I was thinking, That's not boxing. What's going on here? This was like being back in PE at school. I had to adapt to it. I tried cutting him off and landing my shots but every time I got close to him, he just hugged me. At the weigh-in, we had come in at the same weight, but twenty-four hours later I was carrying more, and I think he saw the size and shape of me and decided not to get stuck in. His game plan appeared to be to survive the fight, avoid the punches and not get knocked out. In the first round, I landed a few jabs and at the bell, I went back to my corner and asked Dad what he thought was going on. He told me to stick to what I was doing because I was winning.

There was similar behaviour in the second round,

but I was feeling confident until something awful happened. I threw my right hand, the one that didn't work and was supposed to be completely numb, and I got the shock wave up my arm again. This was not what I was expecting. I actually thought I had broken my hand. All the adrenalin pumping through my body kept me going, but after that my right hand was not as strong as it could have been. I managed to stay focused and not let my mind wander to what this could mean, not just for this fight, but for my future as a boxer. I just had to get through the next few rounds and would worry about it afterwards.

KSI wouldn't let go of me for the whole fight, and every time he clung on, I lost a point. I couldn't understand it. It was his promotion, and he'd paid the referee, so Dad was cross about how the fight was playing out and the crowd were booing too. I just kept focused and carried on. I was willing to engage and wasn't getting the opportunity to. It must have been the worst fight to watch, a six-round stinkfest.

The final bell went. I was sure I had won because I was the only one trying to throw shots, but Dad was convinced I was going to get robbed because I couldn't land my shots as normal. It didn't look as convincing as the Jake Paul fight, and he was worried. I didn't panic, I told him God is good, and to stay positive because we didn't want to put anything bad in the air.

We came to the centre of the ring, the referee holding both our hands and I said a little prayer. The scores were read out and it came down to a majority decision, which meant it was a close fight when I knew it was not. Michael Buffer paused before he announced the winner as '...Tommmmy Fuuurrry'. I erupted. I had won, even though my hand was killing me from the second round onwards, and I was fighting someone who wanted to coast to the end of the fight. Even Mike Tyson's former trainer went on social media to say it was a horrible fight, but I won it. I was over the moon, and I jumped on the rope as everyone went ballistic. I could see Molly crying with happiness and relief.

When I was asked how I felt in the post-fight interview the emotion poured out of me. It had been quite the year and I had just won another massive fight, so I didn't care what anyone else thought.

'I want to thank my Lord and saviour Jesus Christ for this victory tonight,' I said. 'Without him, none of this would be possible. Thank you to everyone in Manchester for turning out. I did it for you, Manchester! I love you! My hometown!' The crowd were going crazy. I will keep that memory of the spectators jumping around for the rest of my life. The interviewer said to me that before the fight I had stated a decision wasn't enough, I had to stop him, so did this result feel like a loss?

'A lot went off in the build-up, I couldn't use my right hand for six weeks. I am not an excuse-maker and the reason I am so emotional is because I am changing my family's life. Fight by fight I am doing it for my daughter. I am trying.' That was the honest truth. It meant everything to me to be able to look after my own. I could hardly hear the interviewer over the cheering. He wanted to know if I thought I had done enough to win the fight before the score cards were read out.

'I fought my absolute heart out and that is all I can do. I said from day one that there will never be another Tyson Fury, I am just trying to be the best Tommy Fury I can be.' The interviewer wanted to know if KSI's performance had surprised me in any way, was he better than I expected?

'Look, he's an awkward man, I will give him that, but I got the victory tonight, and I would like to thank my Lord Jesus Christ. Amen.' The camera panned to KSI, who was shaking his head as the interviewer asked me what I said to him after the fight.

'I haven't spoken to him. At the end of the day, a lot of shit went down in the build-up, it is what it is, he goes his way and I go mine. I am done with all this, I am here to fight and now we go on to the next challenge.' The interviewer got the wrong end of the stick and thought I was done with fighting YouTubers and was going to go back to traditional boxing.

'No mate, I am done with the bullshit. Any of the Pauls want it, I welcome it with open arms. On to the next challenge. Manchester, we can't be defeated!' It went totally wild in the arena. The interviewer turned to KSI to ask for his thoughts.

'Robbery,' he said. He goaded me, wanting to know how many jabs I had landed, which admittedly was pretty hard to do when he was hanging around my neck like he wanted to slow dance with me, but I had got some in.

'I will tell you one thing,' I responded, ready to tell him several things in fact, 'I was pushing the pace, I was throwing the shots . . .' KSI interrupted, saying he was the YouTuber and I was the boxer and he understood I had to win. He did not answer the question of whether he wanted a rematch.

'I felt like I won that,' he said.

'You're a sore loser,' I said as the heat of the moment rose and both our teams began closing in, keeping us apart.

Walking back to the changing room, everyone was congratulating me, shouting out 'Fair play', 'Well done' and 'You smashed it'. BBC Sport were there to interview me, asking how I felt after getting the win. I said great, and a win was a win, against a guy who didn't come to fight, but instead jumped up and down on the spot, wandered in with a shot and then just held on to me. I was still in shock about that. Dad had predicted a scrappy fight, and he was right.

'That doesn't win fights. I was pushing the pace all the time. I was always on the front foot and I was working on the inside. The ref was quick to take a point off me, but he was holding on for all of the fight. I beat him and I beat his promotion.' I was repeating myself in each interview, hammering the point home. I may not have given the performance of my life, but I had just turned twenty-four years old, had come out in front of a packed arena on KSI's promotion and I had won. It showed I had the minerals for it. I said many months ago that I would beat both Jake Paul and KSI within the year and I had done that.

'I beat the two frontrunners and I am at the head of this table now. Crossover boxing belongs to me.' Word.

I was unable to do a wee immediately for the obligatory drug test, so we waited around for a bit. I gave another interview with my dad standing next to me and I thanked him, explaining how it had all started in the garage at the side of our house and then here we were, and it got me emotional all over again. I was physically and mentally exhausted and I wanted to put the controversy of the evening behind me because I was the winner.

The night was over. I was in Manchester and could

have gone out to celebrate – my friends certainly did – but I wanted to go home after ten weeks away. For the first time I didn't want to party after the fight. Molly and I jumped in a car, we ordered pizza and sat on our sofa chatting while Bambi was fast asleep in bed. There was nowhere I would have rather been. I had gone from a rock-star evening of stage, crowds and success to lying in my bed staring at the ceiling, replaying it all in my mind and trying to ignore the fact that my hand was in terrible agony.

We got the win, and KSI had the loss and that will be on his record for ever. There was no conversation between us after the fight. Apparently, he was going around kicking billboards and screaming and saying he had won, and he still claims that to this day. Where I come from, we don't act like that. He hasn't got over it and I seem to be living rent free in his head.

10

Down to Earth

I will never not be grateful. I look for
these realisations and I slow them down to
remind me how far I have come and how
little I really need to be content. Just the
people I love.

After the fight, once all the media and hype had settled down, I could make my family a priority again,
as well as taking a little trip of my own, to my first
Formula One racing event. I had never been before,
and I was invited to Abu Dhabi by Aston Martin.
I loved watching the Grand Prix – it was another
tick on the list of things I had always wanted to do.
I was in the Aston Martin complex when someone

mentioned that the American singer and dancer Chris Brown was performing locally that night. This was a strange fluke. Months earlier, after the Jake Paul fight, Chris had messaged to congratulate me, and I couldn't quite believe it. We texted each other a little and then left it. Fast forward to Abu Dhabi, and here was an opportunity to go to one of his shows. I didn't want to be cheeky, but I also thought, what have I got to lose? So I messaged him asking if it was possible to come, but saying that I completely understood if not. I did not expect to hear back from him and certainly not straight away, but a message pinged back saying he would love to see me. He sent me details of how to attend and I was greeted by his team and taken backstage to see him before watching him perform. He was off-the-scale amazing and afterwards I went out to a party with him to celebrate.

One thing really resonated from hanging out with him that night: he is an incredibly successful guy, but he was as down to earth, likeable, generous and humble as you could imagine. This was so reassuring. He was such a nice person, and it was like being out with a mate I had known for years. Not everyone in the media spotlight is like that. The last message he sent me said, 'Stay in touch, bro,' and I definitely will.

Back at home, Molly and I were really looking for-ward to Bambi's first Christmas. We had lots of festive trips out to take her to see the lights, decorations and winter wonderlands in garden centres. Anything sparkly and we were there! We went to a lot of effort in the house too, dressing it from top to bottom, getting a big tree and buying matching pyjamas. She was mesmerised by it all because there was so much to look at and play with. Of course, Bambi wouldn't remember it, so it was more for us, but we wanted to treasure the memories and make it magical for our little family.

We changed our usual Christmas holiday routine slightly, so on the twenty-third the three of us drove to Molly's mum's and spent a couple of days there. Bambi loved being in the centre of it all. On Christmas morning, I dressed as Santa and Bambi was in a Mrs Claus Babygro because putting your baby in themed outfits is the law when they are little, and we went downstairs to open some presents. She did a good job of ripping the paper and we took loads of photos. About midday, I got my stuff and drove to Manchester to celebrate with my family. I had spoken to Mum and Nana the week before and they said they were thinking about doing something different this year and why didn't we go out? How would we plan that the week before Christmas, I wanted to know! I told them they could have told me sooner, but I was up for a challenge. Amazingly, Mottram Hall, where

I had trained earlier in the year, came up trumps. The owner has become a good friend and he said not to worry, he could organise a private dining room for us. It was brilliant. There was a big Christmas tree, our own waiting staff, music, delicious food and drink, and we had the best time together. It felt good for Mum and Nana not to have to do all the cooking like they always do; I was really glad they got a break.

Later that night I went back to my parents' house to stay the night in my old bedroom. Mum was so happy to have Roman and me there; she said it was lovely to have both sons under her roof and she could sleep in peace. Now I am a dad, I understand exactly what she meant, even though it will be a long time before I have an empty nest. This was my first night back in my old room since I had come out of *Love Island* and I was a few beers deep, so I sat on the bed, emotional about how much had changed since I had lived here. Now I had a baby, a fiancée, a house and a car. On the bed-side table, where I used to put my glass of water, there was a nice watch. And I had smart clothes hanging on the back of the door. I will never not be grateful. I look for these realisations and I slow them down to remind me how far I have come and how little I really need to be content. Just the people I love.

On Boxing Day, I woke up after the best sleep and went down to Heathrow to meet Molly and Bambi because we were flying out to the Maldives. It was our first time taking Bambi on a long-haul flight, but we were all together and she was an absolute angel. Even the flight layover didn't faze her. The airline staff were great and came around with a Polaroid camera to take family photos of us on the plane. Thirteen hours later we were in the Maldives.

It was the perfect opportunity for us to escape and think about the year we'd had. We had a wonderful time there, despite the weather not being exotically fabulous (it rained a lot), then we decided to hang around in Dubai on the way home. We had five blissful days staying in our favourite hotel, Jumeirah Al Naseem and took Bambi to a water park; she was too little to go on the slides, so she watched Mummy come down some instead. Her favourite part was the ice cream. We came home a happy threesome.

And just like that it was Bambi's first birthday. How had a year gone so quickly? She had been a tiny baby curled up on my chest and now she was crawling everywhere, shouting, laughing and obsessed with our two cats, Eggy and Bread. They were less impressed. I went to bed the night before her birthday feeling like a little kid myself and so excited for her. For the first time in a year, I was watching the monitor and willing her to wake up in the morning. Normally I think, Oh please stay asleep for just another five minutes! But

I wanted to take her downstairs and get her into it. She was in a great mood and opened some presents in the morning, then we went for a walk, she had a nap and we got ready for her party. We got her a few nice gifts but didn't spoil her; it was really about having our family and close friends over. Bambi, in her princess party dress, was surrounded by lovely people and other kids for her to play with. She is a very sociable, happy little girl and she loved the afternoon. We did too and had laid on a full spread of cheeses, crackers, salami, fruit, cakes and lots of treats which everyone tucked in to. It was a perfect celebration for a first birthday and Molly made a brilliant cake from a recipe in the cake book that her mum had used for her birthdays when she was little. I love that tradition and she is going to do it every year. Everyone had left by about 6.30 p.m., Bambi had a birthday bath, and she was fast asleep by 7 p.m., partied out. Molly and I snuggled on the sofa together and reminisced about her first year while looking back over photos. Bambi woke up the following morning wondering where everyone had gone! We will forever remember her first Christmas and birthday.

The next thing in my diary was necessary but I was dreading it. I had been putting off surgery on my hand for five years, but after my last fight, it was clear I couldn't wait any longer. The operation had been booked in a few days after Bambi's birthday and I was feeling a bit scared about the general anaesthetic as I had never had one before. Molly drove me to hospital early, ready for the 9 a.m. op, and they started to get me prepped. I rang Molly in a panic about what I had committed to, but she said all the right things and the medical staff around me were comforting.

The reconstructive surgery on the middle knuckle of my right hand took a couple of hours while the surgeon dealt with my snapped ligaments and tendons and the damage I had done to the bone. I woke up with my hand bandaged, feeling a bit woozy but all right. The surgeon said that while it had been a successful operation, he had been doing these for boxers for over twenty years and this was easily the worst injury he had ever seen. I don't think he could believe I had still boxed with it, and for a man like him to say that was worrying. It made me wonder if I would ever be able to fight again and he reassured me that everything signalled that I should. However, if I hadn't had the op and had fought again, it would have likely caused irreversible damage to my hand and my career would have been over. This was sort of comforting.

It was sobering to realise how serious my injury was and how much I had to overcome in the fights. I was supposed to stay in hospital overnight, but the bed was a bit short for me and even though I was dazed and woozy, I just wanted to go home. The nurse asked if I was hungry as I hadn't eaten since the night before and I realised I was starving, so I asked for a tuna mayo sandwich and water and – one more thing – when could I leave? She looked at me like I was crazy because I had just come out of surgery and told me I couldn't go anywhere until I had passed water. I drank as much as I could, had a wee and then they said I could be discharged. An hour later Molly came to pick me up. If I was going to lie in bed all day, I wanted it to be in my own bed. I returned home, one handed, and yes, I may have milked it a bit.

The recovery process is six to eight months and as I write this, I am only a few months in, but I'm hoping by the time you read this I will be back training again. I have to keep the hand moving and I am doing physio a couple of times a week. My knuckle is still badly swollen and I can't make a fist, but I'm doing what I can in the gym. I am just waiting for the surgeon to allow me to ease back into training. If I do well with recovery, he will assess me and make a decision about when I will be ready to fight again. In the meantime, I need to stay positive. As for who I will fight next, there are several contenders including Jake Paul and Conor McGregor, who has called me out. I would love to share the ring with him as I am a fan, I like him, he's a good man. I think our time will come.

After my family, my career is the most important thing to me. I love to train and, as I have already said, if I don't my mental health isn't great. I wake up every day looking for purpose because purpose is everything.

An average day in my life is really a day in Bambi's life. When she gets up, I get up, when she sleeps, I sleep and when she eats, I eat. It's not about me anymore. It's full on and I wouldn't have it any other way. Life revolves around her and if she is happy then so am I; it's impossible to be in a bad mood when I am around her – she always manages to lift my spirits. It is the most amazing feeling when she smiles at me. We are up at 7.30 a.m. and straight to the kitchen for breakfast – like father, like daughter! I will usually make a smoothie for myself before breakfast and am strict at weighing ingredients so I can control my calorie intake. I am often asked what smoothies I like and one of my favourites consists of 100g oats, 50g frozen berries, two eggs, 100g yoghurt, 30g protein and a slug of semi-skimmed milk, all blitzed in the blender. I eat a lot of porridge too, with almond milk, honey and a scoop of my daily obsession, protein powder. I have a cupboard full of powders in the kitchen and I like to switch around to avoid the flavours becoming repetitive.

After we have eaten, we play with Bambi's toys

and then get ready for the morning's activity. On a Monday we go swimming, Tuesday is messy play and Wednesday is baby gymnastics and I take her because it means a lot to me to be there as much as I can. We head home for food before Bambi settles down for a post-lunchtime nap around 12.30 p.m. This is the ideal time for me and Molly to pick up on any work, phone calls, emails or house stuff, although I admit I may have a quick snooze if I'm not too busy. Bambi is up by 3 p.m., bright as a button, ready for big cuddles and to play with her toys. She has a snack, and we hang out together, playing on the carpet, or we pop out until her tea around 5 p.m. By 6 p.m., I am running her bath which she loves to splash around in, then it's a warm bottle of milk, reading bedtime stories and lights out by 7 p.m. I know this is a regimented approach, but it works for us and most of all it works for Bambi. She knows where she is with a routine, and we know what she needs. It's a personal choice – what's right for our family may not be right for others.

Once Bambi is asleep, my working day starts. We have converted the garage into a gym, so I get into my running kit, take the baby monitor with me if Molly is working, and pound on the running machine for several miles. The length and variety of my session will depend on where I am in my training. When I'm not in a training camp, I still make exercise the focus of my day. I will often go to Tyson's gym in Morecambe in the evening, whether he is there or not. I may head over for a session on the pads; he will turn up and surprise me and before I know it, we are body sparring together for six rounds. What was going to be a solid session turns into an elite experience. Or I do a session of technical training with Roman doing drills including skipping, footwork, leg conditioning and practising skills that help with hand and foot coordination, keeping me fresh and ready. After exercise, I jump in the shower before dinner.

I used to take a break after each fight, to relax and enjoy myself. I would stop exercising, eat and drink whatever I wanted and bask in the freedom of not being in a training camp. As I have got older, with more experience under my belt, I realised that this attitude didn't work for me. It is just asking for trouble. After a couple of weeks, my mental health would begin to take a dive and then I would eat and drink more as a comfort, creating a vicious circle of neglect. I would always end up unhappy and wonder why. Now I am very careful not to slip back into those ways. I may take a day or two off, and I am always up for a delicious treat, but I get back in the gym and keep my fitness at a good level. Training is so good for my head – forget boxing, it's the workout that benefits me mentally, whether I have a fight coming up or not. So now I keep to a routine, go to the gym, stick my phone in the locker so I can escape the world and exercise. An hour later I feel on top of the world.

I'll be honest, I'm still not a natural in the kitchen unless it's porridge and scrambled eggs, so I am thankful that Molly is a great cook and baker, and she will often make dinner (although I am not a massive fan of her stew). However, since I started my brand-ambassador role with Marks and Spencer, things are looking up. When they approached me to work with them, I already felt like I knew them because my nana would take me in there as a child and get my school uniform and pants, so it was a pleasure to be associated with this British institution. I film regular food videos with a lovely team and their brilliant chef, Russ, teaches me a new dish in the process so now I can cook chicken, salmon, steak and pasta. It's a solid start.

After we've eaten, we head for the sofa or bed and watch TV before lights out. I always sleep really well. My life is like this ninety per cent of the time and I love it; I want to catch every single minute of Bambi's childhood if I can. The rest of the time I am away for work, either travelling or in a training camp, and I love that too, but my and Molly's favourite time is when the three of us are pottering through the daily routine and enjoying hanging out. It's such a laugh to do it together. We try to make sure our schedules don't clash so I am not away when Molly is, but on the rare occasion when that is not possible, we have help from family including our mums and Molly's sister, which is a godsend. This also means Bambi gets social time with other members of the family, which she absolutely loves.

When I am away, I miss the daily routine the most. Getting Bambi up in the morning, having breakfast, making her laugh and seeing her change with every day that passes. She won't remember this time, but I make sure we do a lot together because nothing comes before her. I don't want to fast forward, but I can't wait to see her as a toddler, on her first day at school and becoming a teenager. There are so many adventures ahead of us. When she gets older, I want her to come everywhere with me; we will have so much to do and see, and I know life will just get better and better.

I used to say I wanted ten children, but that was before I had one and now I think this may be a bit of a stretch. Molly was horrified by the idea. She was thinking more like two, so I am hoping we can meet in the middle at four. She did suggest three, but then how would it work if we all got on a rollercoaster together? Someone would have to sit on their own! This is the sort of random stuff that pops into my head.

Having one is an absolute blessing and I really don't want to push our luck, so we will see what the future brings.

Living with my soulmate, Molly, has been the best because we are completely ourselves with each other. We laugh a lot together, she thinks I am funny and I cheer her up when she is feeling a bit down. We also bicker every day, often around who is the messiest. Molly says I am uber tidy for about ten per cent of the time when I have a manic cleaning session and throw everything away. As for full-blown arguments, we probably have one of those a month and Molly usually extends the olive branch first, so we make up pretty quickly. I think this is a fairly normal relationship. What is less enjoyable are the periods of time when we are apart, the longest being when I am in training camps, but this is the job and we get on with it. We don't have a choice.

Molly and I are very lucky to be invited to amazing events, parties and trips away, but we are careful about how much we accept and our social life at home is low key. We love going to the cinema and munching through popcorn and a bag of pick 'n' mix – that's a great night out. We don't go to lots of fancy restaurants – I'm happy with a Five Guys and I am a big fan of a McDonald's breakfast wrap and hash browns. There is nothing nicer than popping out, with Bambi in the pram, and walking down to the coffee shop or heading to the retail park and looking around B&M Home Store for a good bargain.

If I ever have a few hours to myself, I head to the Lake District. I love getting out into nature, walking, cold-water swimming or standing under a waterfall being immersed in the natural world around me. There is nothing like climbing a big hill or a mountain – I climbed Snowdon in 2018, albeit with the wrong footwear – and taking in an awesome view. Like many people, my phone is constantly pinging with messages, emails and stuff I have to do, so whenever I get an opportunity to ignore it and get out into the countryside, I do. It means I'm able to breathe, and I rarely see other people. As much as I love a hot-weather holiday somewhere exotic – and I very much do – if I had to choose my top destination, it would be walking around the lakes and hills an hour or so from me. The landscape, and the sense of wellbeing I get from being part of it, is invaluable.

11

Champion Mindset

*My brother and my name won't keep
me standing, and won't save me from a
knockout. I have to get on the road in the
pitch black, put the miles in, step in the
ring, take the punches, stand firm on my
feet, cope with the bloody nose and not
complain about the broken ribs.*

I was recently invited to speak at a conference in Abu
Dhabi about what a champion mindset is and how
to nurture it. It was an honour to be asked and it
didn't take much planning to know what I was going
to say, because I have had this mindset for as long
as I can remember, all the way back to when I was

277

a seven-year-old sitting on the carpet at school. My outlook is as much a part of me as my hair, fingernails and height, which is to say, it runs in my blood and it's deep in my bones. It has led me to success, and it has dug me out of a pit of despair. Without it, I know I would be nowhere.

There was a mix of people and professions at the conference, all brought together by a shared attitude that we were keen to compare notes on. It is not just athletes that possess this particular combination of skills; it is important to have a champion mindset in any job, in any industry, if you want to do your best and climb the career ladder. It is about working hard and realising your dreams, and it's no surprise that a negative outlook won't get you very far. So, what does it take to have a champion mindset? Let me share what I have learned to date.

A significant part of building this mindset has to do with having the right people around me: my family, my friends, my training team and my management all join together in support and with my best interests at heart. My first inspiration was and always will be my dad. He was a boxer who reached number eight in the country back in the eighties. Things were different in those days and there was no money in the sport then. While we can now earn a proper living from boxing, Dad was only making a couple of hundred quid for a fight, and he had to pay people out of that. He got to British and European level, and that was without the sort of dedication and infrastructure we have now.

He had to feed the family, so he would be out all day roofing, tarmacking, whatever work he could get his hands on, and then box in the evening for extra cash. Before I was born, he got to a great standard without really training, with fifteen professional fights under his belt, and he fought unbelievable people who went on to be world champions. Nowadays, Tyson and I will go into ten-week training camps, commit our whole life to the process and leave our families at home, but our dad didn't have that opportunity when Tyson was small. His training entailed going for a run down the road and hitting a bag in the shed – that was it. It is incredible to think he got as far as he did and I think if he'd trained as we train now, he could have been a world champion too. At the time, he couldn't afford to sacrifice everything for so little financial reward.

Dad is there for all his boys, whether we box or not, and for those that do he knows how we feel, he gets it, because he has been in the ring. I owe everything in the boxing world to my dad. When we were working away in the garage he would say, 'We will get to the top.' And he was right. I have ten professional fights to my name and the last couple were two of the biggest fights ever, they were mega fights, so effectively we have done it. He got me there. From a garage in Salford – hitting a bag, doing press-ups on the concrete and running up and down the stairs out the back – to a packed Manchester Arena, and that is some leap in a relatively short space of time.

Dad guides my career, he makes things happen and he is the reason I get what I get for a fight, through his negotiation and deal making. Never once has he taken a pound off me. He will get the deal and support me to the win, but he doesn't do it for money. He will devote ten to twelve weeks of his time while we are training for no reward, just so he can see us succeed. There is complete trust between us, and I know I won't come to harm while Dad is around. He's not there for money, fame or publicity, he's there because he wants to protect me and see me do well. I had my first professional fight with him, and I will have my last one with him too. I will finish my career with him. I won't have any other trainer, even though I have been approached by people offering to work with me and promising the moon on a stick. My dad and I have done it from the ground up.

Then there are my brothers, who have all been there for me too, those who don't box and those who do. If one of us is doing well, then the rest of us celebrate it. Roman and I grew up training, wrestling and sparring together from an early age; we have always been incredibly close. As the youngest, I looked up to him and couldn't wait to be old enough to follow in his footsteps, whether it was on the rugby pitch or in the gym. Now he is a professional boxer too, and we are there for each other's fights, supporting in training camps and cheering ringside.

Recently, I went out to Saudi Arabia to watch Roman in his fourth professional fight. He is at the beginning of his career and did incredibly well against an opponent who was much more experienced than him. Officially, the boxer only had two fights to his name so they should have been well matched, but it turned out he had been in around forty kickboxing fights too. Although it was a tough fight, Roman won every round and was victorious. He was on the same bill as the Anthony Joshua fight against Francis Ngannou which meant there was a lot of heat around it. There has been a huge amount of rivalry between Anthony Joshua and my family, but you can't criticise a good performance and Anthony dismantled his opponent; he was punch perfect.

I had arrived earlier in the week to join Roman for his fight-week training, and Dad and Tyson were there too. There is a lot of money in Saudi, and they spend a fortune on hospitality, making it an enjoyable place to visit. We pop to the shopping malls, go out for fantastic food, stay in nice hotels, enjoy good weather and often see sports stars, actors and celebrities doing the same. The country makes a big deal of boxing fights and knows how to throw a show around, going to extreme lengths to promote events. I always feel like I am on holiday there and my experience of the place has only ever been a good one, carrying memories of great times with my brothers.

Tyson and I speak most days and check in to see how the other one is doing. We always try to make each other's fights and spend many hours together in training camps. There isn't an inch of competitiveness between us, just loyalty and support. Tyson is the superstar of the family. I have always looked up to him. When our brother Hughie turned professional at eighteen, Tyson helped him, picked the right opponents for him and they trained together until Hughie stopped boxing because of bad eyesight. Tyson has been the same with me and he continues to mentor me and keep in touch with what I am up to. He has always been a good older brother to have on my side.

I learned a lot from my mum and nana too. They are strong, brilliant women, who have faced adversity and continued undaunted. Without Mum driving me to the gym, or both of them cheering me on from the rugby touchline, putting a hot meal in front of me and surrounding me with love, I would not have been able to build the mindset that has served me so well. Mum could have buckled when Dad was sent to prison, but she got us all through that time, in a way that made the ordeal easier to cope with. With Dad absent, it was a solo ride; nobody came into the boiler room in the morning to get me up and make me go running, that was down to me. I was the one who set my alarm every single night for a 4 a.m. start and I was the one who got myself up and out. There was no point making excuses because the only person I would have been kidding was myself.

Glory in boxing begins and ends with an undefeatable mental attitude. Anyone can hit the bag, skip and run every morning, but not everyone can step into the ring. If I hadn't persevered, I wouldn't be where I am now. There were no guarantees that it would be worth it, in fact the opposite, because nobody expected another winning Fury. I kept going, even when I sat on the bus, my tired forehead against the window, looking out at the grey world with rain lashing down and wondering if I was crazy to pursue this dream. On my darkest days, I questioned what I was doing and if I should have listened to my teachers after all. I didn't have a pound to my name, there were holes in my shoes, and I wore joggers with rips in. I could have given up, but I didn't. I could have turned the alarm off, rolled over and gone back to sleep, but I didn't. I knew I wouldn't get anywhere without perseverance.

In recent years, I have bumped into a few old teachers and classmates from school and I get the same reaction. It's a sort of shocked and begrudging acknowledgement of what I have achieved and several 'how did you get here?' comments, like I got lucky. Like I won the lottery, or success was bestowed on me by a genie or I found good fortune in a hedge.

I don't think anyone believed I would be where I am now, although people are always telling me to my face or through social media, that I wouldn't be anywhere if it wasn't for my brother being heavyweight champion or my family name opening doors for me, and even though I am used to this, it still infuriates me. Just because of who Tyson is, doesn't mean I didn't have to work for my success. He doesn't train for me, get in the ring instead of me, fight my fights or take the abuse for me; I do, and I deserve this. My brother and my name won't keep me standing, and won't save me from a knockout. I have to get on the road in the pitch black, put the miles in, step in the ring, take the punches, stand firm on my feet, cope with the bloody nose and not complain about the broken ribs. A name on paper and a build-up to a fight is one thing, but once I am through those ropes and fighting, it won't carry me. I get so much stick about this – the ratio of negative comments far outweighs the positive – but I don't care what people think of me as long as I have my family around me. That's a crucial part of the champion mindset: self-belief.

At fourteen I was training harder than a professional. This is what it takes. I was single-minded, passionate and I listened to myself. I didn't spend hours scrolling on my phone. Looking at Instagram wasn't going to teach me what I needed to know. It's easy to look at strangers' posts and see successful people without knowing what it has taken some of them to get there. The trick is not to be afraid of hard work. Be obsessed with something and you will be a success at it. Don't invite failure, but when something goes wrong – because it will – keep showing up. I learned that the hard way. I fell and almost refused to get up at the first hurdle I encountered.

I did it through sheer grit, determination and no excuses. I gave myself the best possible chance. No matter what obstacles are put in your path, you have to find a new way through. My drive is one of my biggest qualities and I don't know if this is nature or nurture, but I am guessing it is a bit of both. Some are born with it and others find it along the way and it has to be protected and given encouragement to grow. It can also be inspired by reading or watching something that resonates and motivates you to change your life.

I have met people this has happened to and it's awe-inspiring – they have never looked back.

I used my legs to get me to the gym and my fists to fight and nobody could tell me I couldn't. I wouldn't take no for an answer. If I hadn't pushed myself when it mattered, I would never have been good enough to get to Ricky Hatton's gym, Ricky wouldn't have given the interview calling me Mr *Love Island* and ITV would not have got in touch. That came at exactly the right moment, when I was open to something different, and it changed my life in every way. It's scary when I think about it like that, but as I have said earlier in the book and often repeat, it's the perfect example of 'what's for you won't pass you by'.

A lot of people watched me on *Love Island* or have seen me win my fights, but they don't know me as a person, and may not know where I have come from and how much I have worked for this life. Yes, I grew up in a renowned boxing family, but that doesn't automatically make me a winner. It's been a struggle to get where I am, and I am not about to take my foot off the gas yet, not for a long time. You never stop learning in boxing, ever, and I know I have a lot more to accomplish. I may have earned the occasional lie-in now, but training and fighting continues to be a slog, whatever level you are at. The other part of my career, the brand collaborations and Instagram posts, feels less like work and more like a privilege and I don't ever lose sight of this. I am unbelievably grateful for the opportunities that arise.

I am still hungry to achieve, to remain undefeated, to win every fight. I need purpose. Yes, some things have changed – I sleep in a different house, there's a bit more money in the bank and I don't have to get two buses and a train to the gym – but the mentality of me being a fighter hasn't altered. The moment it does I will walk away from the sport because I don't want to kid myself or tell myself things that aren't true. If I fall out of love with boxing and don't strive to be the best, to be a winner, then I will move on, but right now my drive is as strong as it has ever been. I am hungry to triumph, to capitalise on the position I am in. I want to make sure my family is secure. There is so much on the line, and I know every opponent I face is trying to take that away from me. They want to be the one to make me fall, to detonate my winning streak and I don't blame them – but I am not going to let that happen.

Positive mental attitude is my default and the thought of failure gets me to the gym. I don't dwell on it because if I do and I think about losing it means I could be welcoming it. I haven't been in this position yet, but at some point in a fight when the chips are down and everything is against me, the same thing that is in Tyson is in me too. I know it will come flooding out of me. It takes the right fight to reveal the inner reserves. When my back is against the wall, and I have been hit and hurt and put down I feel like I have the minerals inside me to get back up and show everyone what I am capable of. I will bite down on the gum shield and go for another round because there is no other option.

I put my life on the line every time I go into the boxing ring. One punch could be the end: I could be in a wheelchair, or worse. That's the reality of the sport. This is what boxers risk with each fight and, while I don't think about it when I am fighting, it doesn't mean I am not hyper aware of the dangers we all face in the ring. It is not a job you do for life and you pray you have a life at the end of it.

Whether I give up boxing, or it gives me up, it's going to happen within the next decade or so. The injury to my hand has made me seriously consider how long I can continue, but in my heart, I am a fighter and when I stop I know it is going to be a tough thing to come to terms with. I won't be someone who retires quietly, takes up golf and gets into gardening, not that there is anything wrong with that (I can see the appeal in my *distant* future). I have lots of ideas about what could be next and how I can use the skills I have gained to head in a new direction, like acting, for example. I am a showman and come alive under the spotlight, so I would love to explore this part of my personality and spend time discovering if it is right for me. I could imagine living the American Dream in LA – Hollywood, baby! – or being near to the home of boxing in Las Vegas.

I have also daydreamed about setting up a small number of gyms under the Fury name, which I would run, rather than becoming a coach as I think I would find it too hard not being the one getting in the ring. That said, I might feel differently if I was training my own daughter or son, like my dad has done with me, but only if that is what they wanted. I don't want to be a pushy parent, and boxing isn't a career you encourage your children into unless they are really keen and are prepared for all the risks associated with it. It wouldn't be my first choice for my children, and I know Molly, like my mum, would struggle to cope with the idea of one of her children being punched in the face.

One of my long-time passions is bodybuilding, which has been a big interest of mine since I was about eleven, but I shelved it because it is not possible to be a boxer and a bodybuilder at the same time. The thought of continuing a training regime and a competitive life really appeals to me after my boxing career ends. Every time I go to LA, I work out on Muscle

Beach, and I am fascinated by the history of the place and those who went before me. Anybody who was anybody trained there, and I follow in their footsteps. I have always looked up to Arnold Schwarzenegger, Jay Cutler and Ronnie Coleman, to name just a few, and I want to get my body in that sort of shape when I stop boxing. As a young boy, they looked like superheroes to me, and I wanted to emulate that.

I am not a boxing world champion, but I have the privileges of one so it's hard to leave Molly and my cosy bed behind and get out in the freezing cold to run. I have to step into the mindset that I have nothing. When I shut the front door I think, I am nobody, I do not have a pound in my pocket, I need to do this run to get somewhere. That's the head space I have to get into, and return to the mind of fourteen-year-old me. I run early in the morning or in the evening, when there are no cars, and I can listen to my music, or just focus on my breathing. On the streets in the dark and the silence, my thoughts can move more easily through my head.

Once you are no longer disciplined, that is when I think you are truly lost. Without discipline you don't have anything. If I don't have a fight planned, I still train at a certain level. There are so many more temptations to distract me now. I always think of a great quote from fighter Marvin Hagler: 'It's tough to get out of bed to do roadwork at 5 a.m. when you have been sleeping in silk pyjamas.'

I remind myself of this regularly. Now I am comfortable and have earned some money, how can I hold onto the hunger to go out there and act like a challenger? I am still the same person even if I sleep in a different place, I have a nice car and I have some money in the bank. Am I still getting punched in the head? Yes. Am I still eating McDonald's? Yes. Am I still wearing cheap hoodies? Yes.

As I have said before, *Love Island* turned my world upside down, or maybe it turned it the right way up, because not only did it catapult my career, it also introduced me to the love of my life and someone who shares my approach. It was a brave decision to go on it, considering I already had a career, but I took the diversion and discovered so much about myself in the process. Never in a million years did I think I would meet my future wife, the woman I was destined to have children with, on a reality programme. Molly didn't come from a rich background either. Everything we have done and accomplished in our lives since the show, we have done from the ground up and side by side. I am so proud of the businesswoman Molly has become too.

Family is the most important thing: the one I was born into and the one I have created. Everything I do is for them – the fights, the pay cheques – to ensure we can live a good life. I come from an old-fashioned background, where we weren't spoiled growing up and neither will I spoil my children, but I want to make sure Bambi is looked after. Molly feels the same way. With every year that passes we work hard at securing our future, and of course having money in the bank makes me feel good. That said, I don't need loads of stuff to be happy. I don't have to drive a fast car or have a flash watch on my wrist or fancy suits in the wardrobe. Although those things are there and they are nice, I don't need them because what makes me happy are Molly and Bambi. A few extra rooms in a house and a bigger TV on the wall don't mean anything without them.

I have never wanted to be famous. I have always wanted to be globally renowned and respected as a boxer, not a celebrity or an influencer. I am not complaining about where I find myself and I recognise all the benefits I have gained through it. Of course, the brilliant stuff outweighs the awful parts, but I am not in it for the fame. That is not my motivation.

As you know now, my religious faith is also a big part of who I am, and while I don't hide it, I don't talk about it as much as I could. It's a very personal part of my journey, but as I get older, I feel more confident about sharing my beliefs publicly, without preaching.

I thank God every day for all that is good and for keeping me level-headed and my feet on the ground. Prayer and the Bible are a valued part of my daily routine and I go to church regularly.

I hope this chapter, and indeed this book, has given you an insight into my champion mindset and what I think we all need to thrive and succeed: the right people around us, self-belief, commitment, perseverance, resilience, purpose, discipline, talent, sheer hard work, composure, the ability not to dwell for too long on past failures or be dazzled by the successes. Being positive and strong minded will get you far in life. If you want to do something, it can be done, it just takes elbow grease. Put the work in, sacrifice things and chase what you want because it's all out there in the world, waiting for you. Lastly, but most importantly, we need love. If we love and are loved we are superhuman, we can do anything we put our minds to.

From where I started in life to where I have got to, it's been a ride, and I am still only in my mid-twenties. It just shows that if you have the vision, you can get a good shot at it. I started my career with dust in my pockets. I envisioned what I could achieve, I grafted for it, and I don't take a single thing for granted. I know I will make mistakes in the future, and I am ready to learn from them. There is so much ahead of me, and I hope I meet it all, bad and good, with everything I have.

I wanted to write this book to show where I have come from, share what I have learned and encourage others to be bold with their dreams. The process of spooling back through my twenty-four years has reminded me how much I have done in such a short space of time and how much I want to do with the life that hopefully, God willing, stretches ahead. It has been a painful process of remembering at times; I have had to relive periods of my life I would prefer not to have gone back to and question my motives and decision-making. I guess you could call it a form of therapy. I have found the evenings, once Bambi is in bed, a good time to delve into my past and get my thoughts down on paper. This book is also the best way to recognise and thank all those who have been with me for some or all of the ride – and you, for wanting to read about my life.

Not many people come out of Salford and do really well, especially when someone has already made it in the family: that type of stuff doesn't happen again. Nothing was ever down for me. Tyson is the famous one in the family. If someone had asked my family who else has got a shot at it, nobody would have said me: I was the youngest, the runt of the litter, and I wasn't meant to do anything or be anyone. Instead, I have gone out and achieved my dream and I am absolute proof that lightning can strike in the same place twice.

The Last Word . . .

Since writing this book, some things have changed for me. You may already be aware of this because of the intense press coverage recently. Luckily, after some swift work from my publishers, we were able to delay the first print run so I could add this epilogue. I am really proud of my book, and I wanted to give it as current an ending as it is possible to have in the world of publishing deadlines.

It has been important to me to share the true story of my life to date, with everything that entailed – my childhood, family, boxing career, being catapulted to fame, falling in love, having a child and my hopes for the future. I have divulged everything between these pages and don't regret a word of it. There is nothing to unravel or rewrite, but I do have something to add and where better than here, a place where I can speak freely and feel safe. In the last couple of weeks, I have felt like my voice has been taken away from me.

Right now, Molly and I aren't together. Things have happened, there was an issue, we acknowledged it, we talked about it and we split up. While it is incredibly difficult and sad for us both, I have such a huge amount of respect and love for Molly. She is the mother of my child and our strong commitment to each other is focused on this joint responsibility. Nothing is more important to us than our gorgeous daughter, Bambi, and we are in constant communication, making sure that what we are dealing with is not affecting her.

At the moment I don't want to go into detail about recent events. It isn't fair to talk about a situation that involves more than just me. My first instinct, as always, is to protect Molly and Bambi, and they are my priority. I am not the only author of our story. We have asked for our privacy to be respected while we get to grips with everything.

When the time is right I may talk about what has happened and the truth of our situation. I haven't figured out how to put it into words yet, but I am sure I will. I hope you understand.

What I can say is that this has been, without doubt, the worst few weeks of my life, following on from a very difficult six months due to my hand injury, surgery and recovery. The reality of separating from someone I love, and the grief that comes with that, stole my appetite and my sleep, and piled on the stress and anxiety in the time since it happened.

While I have been at rock bottom personally, I have also had to contend with a media onslaught, the like of which I have never experienced before. Since we made the announcement, the press has picked apart every detail of my life, making wild accusations and concocting false conclusions. Like being thrown to the lions, there are people who have feasted on my heartbreak and turned it into something I don't recognise.

Following our decision to separate, Molly and I told our families and close friends first, before putting out our own statements. Suddenly the news went from something held carefully between a close-knit group of people to being thrust into the unrelenting glare of the media spotlight. It was everywhere within minutes: TV, radio, online, social media. I was in shock and for several hours I felt like I couldn't see straight; it was overwhelming. I couldn't believe the person they were talking about was me and the relationship they were dissecting was mine and Molly's. It was utter madness.

My phone was red hot from the messages pinging in and notifications popping up, so I turned it off. The only way I could survive the first evening was to distract myself with a two-hour gym session. I decided to tire myself out so much that I would not have the energy to think and I managed to block out the media commotion swirling around me. When I got back, I had a shower and went to bed. I didn't switch my phone on again until the following morning, when it was clear the hysteria was building rather than slowing down. I felt completely numb.

It is the strangest thing when the world knows about your private life and struggles. Everyone discusses what is going on and voices their opinion without having any of the facts. In a time when we talk about being kind to others because we never know what someone is going through, I have had the opposite experience. A lot of people have jumped on the 'I hate Tommy' bandwagon without any evidence. It has been a timely reminder to not take social media seriously. I may have millions of Instagram followers who like my photos, but at a single swipe many turn their attitudes into something negative. There are countless numbers of those, but the nice comments still shine out at me, and I appreciate them.

I understand that Molly and I live our lives in an open, online way, but where are we allowed to draw the line between what is public and what is private? Or are we not in control of that? Is that the media's decision? They build you up and they bring you down.

My every move has been followed by an army of photographers and my motives continually debated in the media, including the clichéd and untrue assumption that I had an affair. I did not. Let me state this here clearly for the record: the allegations around me cheating have been created by the press in line with their own agenda and bear no resemblance to the reality of my situation. I am not the first man to have this mud slung at me and I won't be the last.

There are awful things going on in the world and I am always amazed how many column inches are given to people like me. There have been so many incorrect, defamatory and ugly stories that there is no point repeating them here. Nor was there any value in speaking out publicly – I was worried my words would be taken away from me and twisted. I was under siege, and it didn't feel right to rush in and talk about something so important to me, just to get people off my back. Everyone has said what they think and come to their own conclusions, and when the truth comes out, people will have egg on their faces. I know me. I know my heart. I know what is really going on.

As long as my family and friends know I am a good person, then that's all that matters. They sprang into action as soon as the news was out and made sure I was not on my own for too long. I feel so fortunate to have great people around me who have had a lot of life experience and have passed it on to me. I have an old head on young shoulders.

My dad and my brother, Tyson, have been through worse than this. Dad was in prison during our formative years and Tyson has been at breaking point with his mental health. I have seen firsthand how he was put on a pedestal and just as quickly knocked off, so it isn't unfamiliar to me. It is dangerous to put people under such intense scrutiny and to surmise and to plaster their private lives over the front pages. There is so little responsibility taken for telling a true story when the made-up version is more salacious. It's not personal, it's all about a good story and how many papers they can sell.

My mental health took a dive, and as I went through the emotions of loss and heartache these were joined by the anger, distress and embarrassment from the press fallout. Luckily, I have been blessed with a thick skin. If I wasn't, I am not sure how I would have survived such a public hounding. Outside of my family, there is only one opinion I really care about and that is the big man in the sky. I believe everything happens for a reason and this moment will turn out to be a blessing in disguise. I am beginning to see this as something that I needed to go through. The media onslaught has liberated me from caring what other people think and I couldn't be happier about that particular silver lining.

This is life; it isn't easy. My story isn't a fairy tale. Things get messy and complicated. Earlier in the book I said how I would be ready for the bumps in the road, but I am not sure you can ever be prepared. We think we are doing OK and then suddenly along comes a big curveball. I have experienced a few of these and am learning how to bat them away. These difficult weeks are making me think hard about who I am and the changes I need to make. We find out a lot about ourselves during our lowest times and I am channelling the power of this discovery. It's what I do next that matters and how I come back from this. For my daughter. For my desire for reconciliation. For me.

The operation on my hand and the frustration at not being able to box affected me more than I realised when I wrote about it in an earlier chapter. I had not had a break as long as this from fighting. It has been almost a year, and it has completely thrown me. I found it hard to cope without boxing, having a purpose and a date to get in the ring. It is all I know and, as life crumbled around me, I knew it was imperative to get back to it.

So, I have found myself in the boxing ring again. I am built and programmed to be a boxer, and I am in my prime. It has been a challenging time and as I felt my mental and physical wellbeing slide, I focused on training twice a day and already feel in a better place. It is the one thing for me, above all else, which sorts me out. I am looking after myself, eating well, and as long as I feel good and in control, I genuinely believe the rest will fall into place.

I am strong, fit and healthy and I never take this for granted. Exercise is the best medicine in the world, and it has helped take my mind off the external uproar and quieten the internal noise. A thirty-minute run can change the outlook of my morning and shift my mood. It is guiding me through these strange days. So too are the people I surround myself with, who have known me all my life and are keeping me occupied. Whether it's playing tennis or golf, going out for dinner or to the cinema, I am finding moments of genuine happiness. The best of which is seeing Bambi and taking her swimming, to soft play, out shopping and to the park. Every day we spend time together, just like we have always done.

When I see a problem, I go from dwelling on it to thinking, right, I am in this predicament, what am I going to do about it? How am I going to get through it? I never thought I would experience as much as I have by the age of twenty-five and, as a young man, I have had a lot to contend with. Had you told me I was going to break up with the love of my life and then receive a media battering, I would not have imagined I could get through it, but here I am, facing into the storm and getting out of bed every morning. One of the worst possible things has happened to me and I am still here.

Recently I lost myself for a while and life was harder than I chose to admit, but that's for another time. Right now, it's one step in front of another, taking every day as it comes. I have nothing to be ashamed about. There have been a lot of lies written about me, but I have maintained what I hope is a dignified silence. As the saying goes, tough times don't last but tough people do. I am in a positive frame of mind, and I know what I have to do.

My family mean the world to me and I am looking forward to our future.

God bless.

Tommy
September 2024

Acknowledgements

I believe it is important to say thank you and, when it comes to writing my book, it would have been impossible without a brilliant team of people behind the scenes. So, this is my opportunity to recognise them and show appreciation for their hard work and support.

Firstly, to my absolute world, my beautiful fiancée Molly and our gorgeous daughter Bambi, I dedicate this book and my whole heart to you both. Without you, there is no reason. I can't wait to make more stories together.

To my beloved parents, John and Chantal, for always believing in me, surrounding me in love and encouraging my dreams and to my wonderful grandparents, Dev and Barbara. I would not be the man I am today without you. And Dad, I would not be the boxer I am without you by my side. I owe you everything.

A big shout-out to Roman, Tyson, Hughie, Shane and John Boy for being the best of brothers. So too, Chris Worrall and Kyle Dowarka, my mates from primary school who liked me just as much when I had nothing as they do now.

From the boxing world, I'd like to thank the best role model I could ever ask for in my father. I'd also like to recognise a few people who have helped me along the way – Pat Barret, Ricky Hatton, Kyle Dowarka, Bob Howard, Sunny Dhillon, Brendan Lyons, Andy Foster.

Deepest gratitude to my trusted editor, Tig Wallace, at Little, Brown, who has guided and nurtured my story and the experience of turning it into a book, and to the rest of the publishing team. Bear with me because I want to name check them all – Lucy Brazier, Nithya Rae and Ifrah Ismail from editorial; the designer Ellen Rockell; picture research manager Linda Silverman; and rights team Jess Purdue and Louise Henderson-Clark. So, too, Gemma Shelley and Brionee Fenlon in marketing; and Kirsteen Astor, Katya Ellis and Stephanie Melrose in publicity. Also, Louise Harvey in audio; and Hannah Methuen, Caitriona Row, Rachael Jones, Georgina Cutler and the whole sales team and reps. Phew!

Huge thanks are due to my literary agent Oscar Janson-Smith who has navigated me through this whole process, and finally a massive thank you to the best manager in the world, Jake Lee, who makes all of this possible.

Thank you to my Lord and Saviour Jesus Christ, for blessing me with everything that I have in my life. Without him, nothing is possible. God bless everybody and I hope you enjoyed the book.